D1492511

Cordon Bleu

Baking,
Bread and Cakes

Cordon Bleu

Baking 1

Breads, Cakes and Biscuits

CBC / B.P.C. Publishing Ltd.

Published by
B.P.C. Publishing Ltd.,
P.O. Box 20,
Abingdon, Oxon.

© B.P.C. Publishing Ltd., 1971.

Designed by Melvyn Kyte
Printed in England by
Waterlow (Dunstable) Limited

These recipes have been adapted from the Cordon Bleu Cookery Course
published by Purnell in association with the London Cordon Bleu Cookery
School
Principal: Rosemary Hume; Co-Principal: Muriel Downes
Quantities given are enough for 4 servings.
Spoon measures are level unless otherwise stated.

Contents

Introduction

Home-baking is a little out of fashion in these days of convenience foods. It is possible to fetch fresh bread and cakes daily from the local shops and to many people there seems little point in labouring to produce your own.

But to those who like good food, the commercially produced article cannot compare with the bread, cakes, buns and biscuits it is possible to bake in your own kitchen. And for those who love cooking, as well as eating, there is a creative satisfaction in 'doing a baking' unmatched by any other culinary task. The delicious smell, too, is irresistible and draws an instant audience of would-be tasters eager for a warm scone or a slice of cake fresh from the oven.

For a Cordon Bleu cook with a modern kitchen, with a well regulated oven and good ventilation, baking is no longer the hard work it once was. Just because the oven is hot, it is no longer necessary for the kitchen to be the same temperature — windows can be opened without fear of letting draughts into the oven and disturbing the temperature.

Materials are more reliable, too, and electric beaters and whisks take the arm-ache out of mixing.

Many people believe it takes years of practice to acquire skill in baking. In fact the most important thing is understanding your ingredients. If you take the trouble, as a beginner, to find out what each ingredient contributes to the finished product and what conditions it requires in order to function properly, you will automatically know whether you must put your mixture together quickly, keeping the ingredients cool, or whether you should let it stand between stages in mixing, how far you can 'pre-mix' and so on.

Just remember that all baking depends either on a biological process, if eggs or yeast are involved, or on a chemical reaction, if bicarbonate of soda or baking powder are used. Neither biology nor chemistry can be reversed if you make mistakes ; so think first what reaction you are looking for, then allow your materials to give you a perfect Cordon Bleu baking.

Rosemary Hume
Muriel Downes

7

Breads

There are few things more inviting than the taste and warm smell of home-made bread, yet how many people ever try making it ? It's really very easy to bake your own bread, and the taste is refreshingly different from the processed kind to which we have become accustomed.

Bread is probably the oldest, commonest and cheapest form of manufactured human food. In almost every country it is regarded as a staple food, the centre of the diet and a minimum requirement for existence — even in our own sophisticated society it is the 'bread winner' who is the head of the family and the 'bread line' that separates the poor from starvation. Yet how many of us know how to bake our own ?

Making this basic foodstuff is one of the most enjoyable types of baking. Part of the pleasure comes from the knowledge and feeling that you are dealing with a living substance as the yeast begins to work in the dough. So don't regard this chapter as one exclusively for those who live in out-of-the-way places and cannot buy bread daily — try it yourself, for fun.

Successful bread-making lies in understanding your ingredients and how to use them. Yeast and flour are both of great importance, so below we give you a few pointers about them.

Yeast is a living plant, needing warm and moist conditions in which to grow. It is affected by extremes of temperatures : excess cold will retard or check (but not kill) the growth, while strong heat will kill it completely. This explains why bread dough can be mixed and stored before the rising process either in the refrigerator for a short period or in a deep-freeze for a longer time.

After a long and slow rising process, the risen dough is baked in a hot oven to kill the yeast which has done its work.

Sugar helps yeast to grow, but if creaming it with yeast take care not to overmix as that will reduce its qualities ; just stir in enough to bring it to a liquid.

Salt retards its growth if mixed with the yeast, so it is

9

usually sifted with the flour or dissolved in part of the liquid in the recipe.

The proportion of yeast to flour varies with the type of bread. Household breads use 1 oz yeast to 3 lb flour ; light or milk breads, $\frac{1}{2}$ oz yeast to 1 lb flour ; rolls and buns, $\frac{3}{4}$ oz yeast to 1 lb flour.

The proportion of yeast to flour also affects the time allowed for rising. The smaller the quantity of yeast the longer the rising will take ; the greater the quantity the shorter the time.

You can use either fresh compressed yeast or dried yeast. The former is not always easy to obtain, but you can probably buy some from a baker who bakes on the premises. Full directions for using dried yeast are always given on the tin ; it must soak in some of the liquid from the recipe for a given time before being mixed with remaining liquid and flour.

If you want to store fresh yeast, it will keep in a screw-top jar in the refrigerator for more than a week. For longer periods store in the deep-freeze. If you haven't a refrigerator, press into a small jar or pot until three-quarters full, then invert jar in a saucer of cold water. Yeast will then keep fresh and moist for several days.

Note : in these recipes the amount of yeast specified is for fresh yeast.

Dried yeast may be substituted (usually half the quantity), but it is essential to check the quantity and to read the instructions on the tin.

Flour A special bread flour should be used for white bread. It is called 'strong' flour and has a high gluten content. If you find this impossible to obtain, use plain flour. However, some makes of plain flour are stronger than others, so do ask your grocer's advice.

There are also various grades of flour from fine white to coarse wholemeal for different types of bread and certain firms produce stone-ground flour which is ideal for bread-making.

Stages in bread-making

There are four distinct stages in bread-making.

1 Sponging This helps to speed up the general rising of the dough and produces a fine grain in the finished bread. The flour is sifted into a warm bowl with the salt, a well made in the centre and the total quantity of liquid, with the yeast dissolved in it, is poured in.

Draw in enough flour from the sides of the well to make a thick batter. Liberally sprinkle the top of the batter with flour taken from the sides, cover with a damp cloth and set in a warm place to rise ; a fairly cool airing cupboard or a cupboard in a warm kitchen is suitable, where the temperature is 75°F-80°F.

Leave for about 15-20 minutes, or until bubbles start to break through on the surface, which indicates that the batter has started to rise. The batter or sponge, as it has now become, is ready for the next stage.

2 Rising The rest of the flour is then drawn into the spongy

Sponging : the yeast liquid is worked into the warmed flour and salt

After kneading, the dough is transferred to a greased bowl to rise

Remaining flour is worked in, then the spongy dough is kneaded well

When dough is doubled in size, turn out of bowl on to a floured board

dough which is kneaded well on a board or table and transferred to a greased bowl. Turn the dough over in the bowl so that the top surface is lightly greased. This will prevent a skin forming.

Cover the bowl with a damp cloth. Set in a warm, draught-free place until double in bulk. A steamy atmosphere helps the rising and the temperature should be between 70°F-80°F. The dough is then ready for shaping.

3 Proving This next stage is a short period of rising carried out after shaping dough, when it is put in a slightly warmer place than for general rising ; for example over the stove or in a warming drawer, at about 80°F-85°F, and left there for 10-15

11

minutes until the dough begins to swell.

4 Baking Immediately it is clear the dough is rising, the loaves or buns (in their loaf tins or on baking sheets) should be put into a pre-heated oven. As a general rule all yeast mixtures are baked in a hot oven, but if the dough is rich the temperature is lower.

Shape the dough as wanted and then line it into greased bread tins

Leave tins in a warm place to prove the dough before baking

Kneading the dough to make bread light is an important stage of bread-making. To knead by hand, take the edge of the dough and pull it into the centre with the fingers. Push out again with the heel of the hand so that dough 'rolls' on the board. Kneading is done with both hands with a rhythmical movement. If you have an electric mixer, kneading can be carried out at a slow speed using the dough hook.

For a **crisp crust** leave the loaves as they are. For a **softer crust** rub with buttered paper ; when turned out, cover with a cloth for 5-10 minutes.

Ordinary bread is made with water, which gives a crisp crust. Light bread, such as teacakes, milk bread and buns, is made with milk and a small quantity of fat, which give a soft crust and a spongy texture to the crumb.

Baking temperatures

Type of Bread	Electric and solid fuel	Gas
Bread	425-400°F	7-6
Rolls	425°F	7
Buns (small)	450°F	8
Tea cakes	450-425°F	8-7
Bun loaf, brioche and savarin	400°F	6

Household bread

2 lb plain flour
1 dessertspoon salt
$\frac{1}{2}$-$\frac{3}{4}$ oz fresh yeast
$\frac{1}{2}$ teaspoon caster sugar
1 pint water
lard (for greasing bowl)

2 loaf tins, 9 by 5 by 3 inches

Method
Sift flour with the salt into a warm mixing bowl. Cream yeast and sugar, add to the water.

Make a well in the centre of the flour, warm the liquid, pour it in and draw in enough flour to make a thick batter. Sprinkle with flour from the sides, cover with a damp cloth and leave in a warm place 15-20 minutes.

When bubbles have broken through the floured surface, work up to a dough with the hand. Turn on to a floured board or table and knead until dough is no longer sticky. Dust occasionally with flour. Put back into a clean and lightly-greased warm bowl, turn dough over and make a shallow cross-cut on the top. Cover with the cloth and leave to rise 1-1 $\frac{1}{2}$ hours until double in bulk. Grease tins and set oven at 425°F or Mark 7.

Turn dough on to floured board and knead lightly for a few seconds. Then cut in half, shape and put each piece into a tin. Stand these on a baking sheet, cover with the cloth and prove for 10-15 minutes. Bake for 35-40 minutes in pre-set oven. Lower heat after 20-25 minutes to 400°F or Mark 6.

When well browned and shrinking slightly from sides of tins, tip loaves on to a rack to cool. Tap bottom of loaf ; if it sounds hollow, the bread is done.

Light bread

1$\frac{1}{2}$ lb plain flour
1 rounded teaspoon salt
good $\frac{1}{2}$ pint milk
2 oz butter
$\frac{3}{4}$ oz fresh yeast
1 rounded teaspoon caster sugar
1 large egg (beaten)
lard (for greasing tins)

To finish
beaten egg and $\frac{1}{2}$ teaspoon salt
  (for glazing)
poppy seeds (optional)

1 large loaf tin, or 2 smaller ones

Method
Sift flour and salt into a warm bowl. Warm the milk slightly, add butter and stir until dissolved. Cream yeast and sugar together and add to the luke-warm milk with the egg.

Make a well in the centre of the flour, pour in the liquid and mix with the hand to a soft dough. Then knead well until smooth and elastic. Put to rise, covered with a damp cloth, until doubled in bulk (about 1 hour). Turn on to a floured board and knead lightly.

The dough is now ready for shaping and baking in a greased tin, or shaping into a twist. Or make 1 loaf and use remaining dough for rolls. Prove in usual way then brush with beaten egg mixed with salt.

The loaves, twist or rolls can be sprinkled with poppy seeds or left plain.

Bake loaves or twists for 40-45 minutes at 400°F or Mark 6 ; rolls for 15-20 minutes at 425°F or Mark 7.

Wholemeal bread

3 lb coarse wholemeal flour
2 tablespoons salt
1¼ oz fresh yeast
1 tablespoon Barbados sugar
1¼ pints milk and water (mixed)
lard (for greasing tins)

2 loaf tins, 9 inches by 5 inches by 3 inches, or sandwich tins (optional)

Method
Sift salt thoroughly with flour in a warm mixing bowl and make a well in the centre. Cream sugar and yeast together, warm the milk and water, add to yeast and stir well to mix.

Pour liquid into the well and with your hand mix the flour into the liquid, gradually drawing it from round the sides of the bowl. It should be a soft dough, so quantity of liquid may need slight varying. Cover bowl with a thick cloth and leave to rise in a warm place 1-1½ hours.

Set oven at 400°F or Mark 6. Turn dough on to a floured board; knead until it leaves board and hands are clean. Divide dough into two, knead each piece until there's no trace of stickiness.

Shape each piece into a round loaf and put on a floured baking sheet, or into greased tins, but do not let sides of loaf touch the tin. Prove for a further 30 minutes. Bake in the pre-set oven for 1 hour.

Fine wholemeal bread

1½ lb wholemeal flour
8 oz plain white flour
1 dessertspoon salt
1 oz butter, or lard
¾-1 oz fresh yeast
1 teaspoon caster sugar
¾-1 pint warm water
lard (for greasing tins)

2 loaf tins, 9 inches by 5 inches by 3 inches, or sandwich tins (optional)

Method
Mix flours and salt together in a bowl, rub in butter or lard. Continue as for wholemeal bread.

Watchpoint Wholemeal flour absorbs slightly less liquid than a finer flour; this should be taken into account when mixing the dough.

Cottage loaf

Make as for household bread (see page 14), but divide dough in two pieces, one twice the size of the other. Knead each piece lightly into a bun shape. Set the large piece on a baking sheet, put the small one on top and push your finger right through the centre down to the sheet. Prove and bake as for household bread.

Grant (or granary) loaf

3 ½ lb English stone ground
   wholewheat flour
1 dessertspoon salt
1 oz yeast
1 oz sugar (preferably Barbados
   cane sugar)
2 pints 4 fl oz water (at blood heat)

3 loaf tins (2-pints capacity)

This bread, created by Doris
Grant, a pioneer in the whole-
foods movement, is excellent
for sandwiches. Chill briefly
before slicing, to prevent
crumbling. It should keep moist
for 5 days as fresh bread and
can be used for another few
days as toast. Remember that
the wholewheat dough must
not be kneaded and only
requires a few minutes to mix.

Method
Grease the inside of the tins and
warm them well.

Mix the salt and flour in a
large basin and warm this in
the oven or above a low gas
flame, so that the yeast will work
more quickly.

Crumble the yeast into a large
basin, add the sugar and ¼ pint of
the water. Leave for 10 minutes
to froth up, then stir to dissolve
the sugar. Pour this yeasty
liquid into the basin of warm
flour, add the rest of the warm
water and stir the whole with
a wooden spoon until the flour
is evenly wetted. The dough
should be so wet that it is
slippery.

Spoon the dough into the
warmed tins, put them about
2 feet above a low gas flame
(or in the oven while it is
warming up to 375°F or Mark
5). Cover with a cloth and leave
for about 20 minutes ; the
dough will rise by about one-
third. Then bake in the pre-set
hot oven for 45-60 minutes.

Note : if the bread is not
allowed to rise sufficiently
before being baked, it will be
close in texture, but if allowed
to rise too high it will be spongy
and will not keep moist for so
long.

Refrigerator rolls

6 oz potatoes
1 lb plain white flour
2 oz butter
1 teaspoon salt
$\frac{3}{4}$ oz fresh yeast
1 dessertspoon caster sugar
$\frac{1}{2}$ pint milk and water (mixed)
1 large egg
beaten egg mixed with $\frac{1}{2}$
    teaspoon of salt (for glazing)
    — optional
lard (for greasing)

The potatoes help the fermentation and make these rolls especially light. The dough keeps very well in the refrigerator, or for longer in the deepfreeze, and a little at a time can be used from this stock.

Method

Boil potatoes in their skins. Peel and crush well with the masher, or put through a sieve. Put into a warm bowl, sift in the flour, rub in the butter and add salt.

Cream yeast with the sugar, warm the milk and water and add to yeast together with the beaten egg. Pour into a well in the flour mixture and work up to a dough. Knead until the dough has no trace of stickiness, dusting occasionally with a little flour.

If storing this dough, put it in a basin covered with a plate in the refrigerator. After 12 hours the dough will have risen to the top. Push it down and turn it over. Make a cross-cut on the top, cover and leave until wanted. It will keep for at least a week in the fridge. If dough rises to top of the bowl, push it down with the back of your hand.

When wanted for use, knead lightly and leave to rise in a warm place until double in bulk. The longer the dough has been kept, the longer rising time it will need here.

If using immediately, turn into a greased basin and leave to rise until double in bulk (1-$1\frac{1}{2}$ hours). Then knead lightly and shape into rolls. Prove and bake on a greased baking sheet in the oven, pre-set at 425°F or Mark 7. Brush with beaten egg mixed with salt if you like a glazed finish.

Baps

1 lb plain flour
1 teaspoon salt
½ pint milk and water (mixed)
2 oz shortening, or butter
½ oz fresh yeast
1 teaspoon caster sugar

This is a quick, light bread, suitable for either breakfast or dinner rolls.

Method

Sift flour with salt into a warm bowl. Warm the milk and water, add the fat and stir until dissolved. Cream yeast and sugar, add to the liquid and pour it all into the centre of the flour. Mix to a soft dough and knead until smooth and elastic.

Cover with a damp cloth and leave to rise in a warm place for 1-1½ hours. Set the oven at 425°F or Mark 7.

Knead dough lightly on a board and divide into 6 pieces. Roll each piece on a floured board to an oval, or flatten with the heel of the hand. Set on a floured baking sheet, dust with flour, prove and then bake in the pre-set oven for 10-15 minutes. Lower heat slightly after 5 minutes to 400°F or Mark 6. When cooked, the baps should be pale brown in colour.

Buns, scones and soda breads

For tea-time bread we often follow the old Irish tradition of leavening the dough with soda instead of yeast. With its cousin scones (a Scottish name !), this soda bread is very quickly made and for this reason has remained a popular baking recipe. But don't forget that your yeast dough can still be trimmed up for tea-time with the addition of butter and fruit to turn it into a bun loaf.

Bicarbonate of soda is a very fast-acting raising agent, and its leavening properties are quickly expended. Soda bread and scone doughs must therefore be mixed quickly and handled lightly. They taste much better, too, if they are eaten the day they are made ; you shouldn't have any problem with leftovers, though, as they are so delicious straight from the oven that you are unlikely to have many left after tea-time ! If there are a few over, store them in an airtight tin and slice and toast them the next day.

In the old days, soda breads and scones were always baked on a girdle, or griddle, which is a thick, round, iron plate, usually with a semi-circular (half-hoop) handle. This is used on top of the stove and even now, unless you are using the oven for other baking at the same time, it is more economical to use a girdle than to light the oven specially for a batch of scones. Soda breads are usually shaped into a large round with the hands and scored with a knife to mark four three-cornered portions ('farls') ; scones may be shaped in the same way or cut into small rounds, say 2 inches in diameter, before cooking.

General points
The raising agent should be bicarbonate of soda used with an acid such as buttermilk or sour milk. The two together release the carbon dioxide necessary to make bread light.

If neither of these acids are available, and fresh (sweet) milk is used, you will need to add twice the amount of cream of tartar to bicarbonate of soda. A tablespoon of black treacle, which is also an acid, helps rising in this case.

Plain flour is best, but if using self-raising flour, you must still add bicarbonate of soda with an acid. This is because the proportion of raising agent for scone dough should be greater than that of the raising agent present in self-raising flour.

Mixing and handling. Sufficient liquid should be added to dry ingredients to make a soft dough. Avoid any delay between mixing and baking.

Baking. Scones should be baked quickly to prevent them from getting overbrown on the bottom ; cook on shiny, ungreased baking sheets (a shiny surface reflects heat).

If cooked on a girdle, scones or soda bread should be rolled thinner than for baking or they will be too brown before the middle is sufficiently cooked. Cook more slowly on a girdle than when baking.

Watchpoint A girdle must be pre-heated to the right heat. A frequent mistake is to have it too hot at first and in consequence the outside crust becomes too brown, leaving the centre uncooked. This applies especially to bread.

A good test is to sprinkle the girdle with flour ; if this becomes light-brown in colour in 3 minutes, the girdle is at the correct temperature. Alternatively sprinkle a few drops of water on to the girdle. If it is heated to the right temperature, they will dance around. If possible turn loaves or scones once only (this may have to be disregarded if girdle was a little too hot in the first place).

Rich bun loaf

1 lb plain flour
$\frac{1}{2}$ teaspoon salt
$\frac{1}{2}$ teaspoon mixed spice, or
  cinnamon
3 oz butter
7$\frac{1}{2}$ fl oz milk
1 oz fresh yeast
1 rounded teaspoon caster sugar
3 eggs
3 oz currants
3 oz sultanas
3 oz caster sugar
rind of $\frac{1}{2}$ lemon (grated)
1 oz candied peel (finely chopped)
1 tablespoon caster sugar (dissolved
  in 1 tablespoon milk) — for
  glazing
lard (for greasing tins)

2 lb loaf, or cake, tin

Method
Sift flour, salt and spice together into a warm bowl. Rub in the butter. Warm the milk, cream the yeast and the teaspoon of sugar, beat eggs and add all three to milk. Pour on to flour, mix to a soft dough. Knead until smooth, put in a greased bowl, cover with a damp cloth and leave to rise ; this will take about 45 minutes.

Set oven at 400°F or Mark 6. Grease the tin.

Clean the fruit and mix into the dough with 3 oz sugar, lemon rind and candied peel. When well mixed, turn into the greased tin. Cover with the cloth and prove 15-20 minutes, then bake in pre-set oven for 35-40 minutes. When cooked, brush with the sweetened milk and turn out to cool.

Bun loaf

A simple bun loaf can be made from a bread dough with dried fruit, butter, sugar and eggs worked in before proving.

When making a batch of bread use a portion of the dough for this. To 1 lb of dough add 2 oz creamed butter, sugar, 1-2 eggs (depending on size) and dried fruit to taste.

Hamburger bun

2 lb plain flour
1 teaspoon salt
1 pint skimmed milk
1 oz yeast
4 oz butter
2 tablespoons caster sugar
little milk (to finish)

This quantity makes 30-40 buns.

Method
Sift the flour with the salt into a mixing bowl. Warm the milk to blood heat, add the yeast, butter and sugar, and stir until dissolved. Pour mixture at once into the centre of the flour and mix to a smooth dough. Put the dough into a greased bowl, cover with a damp cloth and set to rise in a warm place for 1 hour, or until double in bulk.

Set oven at 425°F or Mark 7.

Turn the dough on to a floured board, divide into equal portions and knead into small balls. Flatten these with the palm of your hand, set them on a greased and floured baking sheet and prove for 10 minutes. Brush the tops with milk and cook for 15-20 minutes in pre-set oven.

While still hot, rub the top of each bun with buttery paper.

Wholemeal scones

8 oz plain flour
large pinch of salt
2 teaspoons bicarbonate of soda
2 teaspoon cream of tartar
8 oz wholemeal flour
4 teaspoons caster sugar
4 oz butter, or margarine, or lard
½ pint buttermilk, or fresh milk
   with 3 teaspoons baking powder

This recipe makes approximately
8 scones.

Method
Set oven at 425°F or Mark 7.
Sift the plain flour with the salt,
bicarbonate of soda and cream
of tartar into a mixing bowl, add
the wholemeal flour and caster
sugar and mix well. Rub in the
fat until evenly distributed, stir
in the buttermilk (or fresh milk
with baking powder) and mix
quickly to a soft dough.
   Turn dough on to a floured
board, divide it in two, knead
lightly and then pat or roll it into
two rounds.
   Cut each round into four and
piace them on a baking sheet,
fitting pieces together to make
two rounds again. Dust with
flour and bake in pre-set oven
for about 12 minutes.

Girdle scones

8 oz plain flour
large pinch of salt
1 level teaspoon bicarbonate of
   soda
1 rounded teaspoon caster sugar
2 oz butter, or margarine, or lard
1 teaspoon cream of tartar with
   ¼ pint buttermilk, or ¼ pint fresh milk
   with 2 teaspoons cream of tartar
1 tablespoon currants (optional)

Girdle, or very thick frying pan

This recipe makes approximately
8 scones.

Method
Heat girdle. Sift flour with salt,
bicarbonate of soda and sugar
into a bowl ; rub in the fat.
Dissolve cream of tartar in the
buttermilk (or fresh milk). Add
currants and buttermilk to bowl
and mix quickly to a firm dough.
   Turn dough on to a floured
board, divide in half and shape
into two rounds, ½-inch thick ;
cut each round into quarters.
Dust with flour and cook on the
hot girdle, in thick frying pan or
direct on a solid hot plate, until
risen and lightly brown (about
5 minutes). Turn and cook on
the other side. Split, butter and
serve scones immediately.

Drop scones

5 oz plain flour
large pinch of salt
2 teaspoons baking powder
caster sugar (to taste)
1 oz melted butter
1 egg
¼ pint fresh milk

Girdle

This recipe makes approximately 30 scones.

Method
Heat girdle over a moderate heat while mixing the batter. Sift all the dry ingredients (plus up to 1 tablespoon sugar to taste) into a mixing bowl, make a well in the centre and drop in egg and melted butter. Add milk gradually and beat well with a wooden spoon.

Grease the girdle very lightly and pour the mixture from the point of a spoon or from a jug, to give perfectly round cakes. As soon as the 'pancakes' are puffed and full of bubbles, and the undersides golden-brown, lift them with a palette knife, turn and brown on other side. Serve immediately or place between folds of a clean, warm tea towel until wanted. Serve with butter and honey or jam.

Potato scones

1½ lb floury, freshly boiled potatoes
salt
6 oz plain flour

Girdle

This recipe makes approximately 12 scones.

These scones, which are different in shape and texture to drop scones, are equally good eaten cold or fried with the breakfast bacon. Made in large farls (large rounds marked in four), they are thin and flexible.

Method
Crush or sieve potatoes on to a floured board. Add salt to taste, work in the flour gradually, kneading it lightly and carefully.

Roll out mixture as thinly as possible. Cut into rounds the size of a dinner plate, then cut each round into quarters. Bake scones on a moderately hot girdle for 7-10 minutes, turning them once only.

Treacle scones

$\frac{3}{4}$ lb plain flour
$\frac{1}{2}$ teaspoon salt
1 teaspoon bicarbonate of soda
1 teaspoon cream of tartar
2 oz butter, or margarine
2 tablespoons black treacle
$\frac{1}{4}$ pint soured, or fresh, milk

This recipe makes approximately 8 scones.

Method
Set oven at 425°F or Mark 7. Sift flour with salt, bicarbonate of soda and cream of tartar. Rub in butter or margarine. Mix treacle with the milk, then stir into the dry ingredients.

Knead the scone mixture lightly on a floured board, then roll out and cut into triangles. Bake in pre-set oven for about 7-10 minutes, or cook on a moderately hot girdle for 7-10 minutes, turning once only.

Soda scones

1 lb plain flour
1 teaspoon salt
1 teaspoon bicarbonate of soda
$1\frac{1}{2}$ oz butter
$\frac{1}{2}$ pint buttermilk, or soured milk (or fresh milk with 2 teaspoons cream of tartar)

2-inch diameter plain cutter

This recipe makes approximately 8 scones.

Method
Set oven at 425°F or Mark 7. Sift flour with salt and soda into a bowl. Rub in butter. Mix quickly to a soft dough with the milk. Turn on to a floured board, knead lightly then roll out about $\frac{3}{4}$-inch thick. Stamp out into 2-inch rounds with a plain cutter or cut into triangles.

Bake on lightly floured baking sheet for 12-15 minutes until risen and golden-brown.

Taking soda scones out of the oven ; they should be well risen and golden

Soda bread

1½ lb plain flour
1½ teaspoons salt
1½ teaspoons bicarbonate of soda
scant 1½ oz butter
about ¾ pint buttermilk, or fresh
   milk with 1 dessertspoon
   cream of tartar

Method

If not using a girdle, set the oven at 400°F or Mark 6.

Sift the flour with salt and bicarbonate of soda into a mixing bowl. Rub in the butter and mix with the milk to a soft dough. Turn the dough on to a floured board and shape into a large round about 2 inches thick.

Score or cut into quarters, place on a floured baking sheet in a circle and bake in pre-set oven for about 25-30 minutes (or cook on a girdle) until the bread sounds hollow when tapped on the bottom.

Fly bread

Bake as for soda bread, adding a handful of cleaned currants to the dry ingredients.

Baking powder bread

Bake as for soda bread, but use self-raising flour.

Brown soda bread

Bake as for soda bread but use half wholemeal flour and half white flour. Bake or cook on a girdle.

Scoring the soda bread into quarters before baking ; it may be cut instead

Testing the soda bread ; if cooked it should sound hollow when tapped

Savoury drop scones

4 oz plain flour
salt and pepper
pinch of cayenne pepper
1 teaspoon caster sugar
2 tablespoons grated Parmesan
cheese
1 egg
2 tablespoons melted butter
¼ pint milk

These scones should be filled at the last possible moment. Following this recipe are three suggested fillings. This quantity will make about 24 scones.

Method

Heat a girdle or heavy frying pan over moderate heat while mixing the batter.

Sift the flour, seasonings and sugar into the mixing bowl. Add the Parmesan cheese and mix well. Make a well in the centre and drop in the egg and melted butter, add the milk gradually, beating well with a wooden spoon. Grease the girdle or frying pan very lightly and pour the mixture from the point of a spoon, or from a jug, to give perfectly round, small scones. As soon as the 'pancakes' are puffy and full of bubbles and their undersides golden-brown, lift them with a palette knife, turn and brown on the other side.

Serve immediately, or place between the folds of a clean, warm tea towel until ready to serve. Do not reheat scones as this would toughen them.

Filling 1

Remove rind and rust from finely cut rashers of 'tender-sweet' streaky bacon.

Stroke out rashers with blunt edge of heavy knife, cut them in half, then spread with French mustard. Roll up and skewer, then grill or bake until crisp.

Put bacon rolls into the scones while piping hot. Curl scones round the bacon and secure with cocktail sticks (see photograph left).

Filling 2

2 oz cream cheese
salt and pepper
1 can (1¾ oz) Danish caviar
squeeze of lemon juice

Method

Season the cream cheese and spread on the hot scones.

Sprinkle the caviar well with the lemon juice and put ½ teaspoon of it in the centre of each scone. Fold over and secure with cocktail sticks.

Filling 3

For a really extravagant cocktail savoury put 1 teaspoon of pâté de foie gras on to each warm scone and fold over. A less expensive way is to use liver pâté, carefully seasoned with a dash of French mustard and a few drops of brandy.

27

Savoury scones

4 oz self-raising flour
salt and pepper
pinch of cayenne pepper
1 oz butter
2 teaspoons chopped chives
$\frac{1}{2}$ egg
2 fl oz milk
little milk, or beaten egg

Plain cutter (1 $\frac{1}{2}$ -inch diameter)

These small savoury scones are good served hot and quite plain to accompany a savoury dip.

Method

Set the oven at 400°F or Mark 6. Sift the flour with the seasonings, rub in the butter and add the chopped chives.

Stir the $\frac{1}{2}$ egg into flour, with enough milk to give a soft dough. Turn on to a floured board and knead lightly to a smooth ball. Roll out to just under $\frac{1}{2}$ inch thick and stamp into 1 $\frac{1}{2}$-inch diameter rounds.

Place the scones on an un-greased baking tray, brush with milk or beaten egg and bake in the pre-set hot oven for 10-12 minutes.

Welsh cakes (or girdle scones)

8 oz self-raising flour
3 oz butter
pinch of salt
3 oz currants
3 oz caster sugar
1 egg
little milk (to mix)
extra caster sugar (to sprinkle)

Girdle

Method

Rub the fat into the flour. Add the dry ingredients, then the egg and milk. Mix into a stiff paste. Roll out, cut into rounds and bake on a girdle over medium heat. When cold, sprinkle with extra caster sugar.

Regional and traditional baking

If not perhaps as rich in regional dishes as France, Britain can boast quite a number of traditional baking recipes that are still made and eaten today, especially in the country districts. Some of them, such as hot cross buns, are linked with certain festivals, while others are derived from local produce or evolved from local customs.

The crumpets, muffins, breads, scones and cakes in this section are all very much regional dishes and make a good addition to a high tea or supper.

Crumpets

1 ½ lb plain flour
1 teaspoon salt
about 1¾ pints milk
¾ oz yeast

4-inch diameter crumpet rings

This mixture makes 18-24 crumpets. They may be cooked on a girdle or in the oven.

Method

Grease the crumpet rings. Sift the flour and salt into a warm bowl. Heat the milk to luke-warm and dissolve the yeast in ¼ pint of it. Make a well in the centre of the flour, pour in the milk and yeast mixture and stir ; gradually add the remainder of the warm milk until a batter the consistency of cream is formed. Cover and leave for about 40-45 minutes to rise.

Set crumpet rings on a hot greased girdle or baking sheet (if using oven). Pour in batter to fill the rings by about ¼ - ½ inch. If cooking crumpets on a girdle, set it on a slow to moderate heat ; when the bot-

Pouring the crumpet batter into rings set on a greased girdle ; cook over slow to moderate heat

toms of the crumpets are nicely brown, turn them and cook for a further 3-4 minutes. Alternatively, cook in the oven (pre-set at 375°F or Mark 5) for about 20-25 minutes.

Watchpoint Crumpets must not be too well browned because they have to be toasted for serving.

Muffins

1½ lb plain flour
1 teaspoon salt
about ¾ pint milk
¼ oz yeast

4-inch diameter crumpet rings

Muffins are made from the same ingredients as crumpets but less milk is used and the mixture is a soft dough, not a batter. They should be cooked on a girdle but can be done in the oven. The same rings are used for both muffins and crumpets. This quantity of dough makes about 12 muffins.

Patting muffin dough into the rings on a floured board before cooking

Method

Prepare as for crumpets (see page 31), but mix to a soft dough.

Once the dough is well risen, divide it into even-sized pieces ; pat these lightly on a well-floured board in the shape of the crumpet ring, putting one piece into each ring.

Set the girdle on a slow to moderate heat and cook the muffins on each side to a light brown. Alternatively, cook in the oven (pre-set at 375°F or Mark 5) for 20-25 minutes. To serve, toast on both sides, pull them apart and butter thickly.

Oatmeal bread

10 oz self-raising flour
5 oz medium, or fine, oatmeal
½ teaspoon salt
4 oz butter, or margarine
1 tablespoon caster sugar
1 egg
6-7 fl oz milk

Method
Set oven at 400°F or Mark 6.

Mix flour, oatmeal and salt together. Rub in the fat, add sugar and the egg, beaten with sufficient milk to make a light scone dough. Turn on to the table or board and pat out into a round about 1-1½ inches thick. Slide the round on to a baking sheet and cut into farls (ie. three-cornered pieces) without separating completely, as is traditional.

Bake in the pre-set hot oven for about 40-45 minutes. Five minutes before they are done, turn the farls upside-down and return them to the oven to finish. Eat like soda bread.

Huffkins

1½ lb plain flour
1 teaspoon salt
2 oz lard
1 oz yeast
1 teaspoon caster sugar
about ¾ pint milk and water (mixed)

These flat oval cakes with a hole in the middle come from East Kent and are made of light bread.

Method
Sift the flour with the salt, rub in the lard and make a well in the centre. Cream yeast with sugar, heat milk and water to lukewarm and add to the yeast. Pour this mixture into flour and work up to a soft dough, adding more liquid if necessary. Knead until smooth, then return dough to bowl ; make a cross-cut on the top and leave to rise for about 1 hour, or until doubled in bulk.

Set oven at 400°F or Mark 6. Take up dough, knead lightly and divide into even-sized pieces (about 3 oz each), shape into oval cakes about ½ inch thick, making a hole in the middle with a finger. Slide on to a floured baking sheet, prove for 10 minutes, then bake in pre-set hot oven for 10 to 15 minutes. Lift cakes from the sheet and wrap in a thick cloth until cold to give a soft crust. Serve with butter and jam, as a teacake.

Revel buns 1
(Saffron buns)

12 oz self-raising flour
pinch of salt
4 oz butter
2 oz currants (cleaned)
2 oz caster sugar
2 fl oz Devonshire cream
1 egg (beaten)
large pinch of saffron (infused in 2 tablespoons hot milk for 30 minutes and cooled)
crushed lump sugar (to sprinkle)

Method
Set oven at 375°F or Mark 5.

Sift flour with the salt. Rub in the butter, then add currants and sugar. Make a well in the centre and in this put the cream, beaten egg and strained saffron-flavoured milk. Mix with a fork to a fairly firm consistency.

Put out mixture, a dessertspoon at a time, on to greased baking sheets. Sprinkle with crushed sugar and bake in preset oven for 15-20 minutes.

Revel buns 2
(Saffron buns)

1 lb plain flour
pinch of salt
$\frac{1}{2}$ teaspoon ground cinnamon
4 oz butter
$\frac{3}{4}$ oz yeast
4 oz caster sugar
large pinch of saffron (infused in $\frac{1}{4}$ pint hot milk for 30 minutes)
6 fl oz Devonshire cream
2 eggs (beaten)
4 oz currants (cleaned)
beaten egg (to glaze)

This dough has to be made the day before it is to be cooked.

Method
Sift the flour with salt and cinnamon, then rub butter into the flour. Cream yeast with a little of the sugar ; when lukewarm, strain on the saffron-flavoured milk and add cream to it. Pour this mixture into the centre of the flour with the beaten eggs. Add currants and knead the mixture. Cover and leave in refrigerator overnight.

Set oven at 375°F or Mark 5. Shape dough into buns and leave to prove for 15 minutes. Then brush tops lightly with a little beaten egg, sprinkle with remaining sugar and bake in preset oven for about 15 minutes.

Sally Lunn

7 ½ fl oz milk
1 oz butter
12 oz plain white flour (warmed)
½ teaspoon salt
1 egg
¾ oz fresh yeast
1 teaspoon caster sugar
1 tablespoon sugar dissolved in 1
  tablespoon milk (for glazing)
lard (for greasing tins)

Two 5-inch diameter cake tins

This is a typical and popular English teacake.

> **The name Sally Lunn** is said to originate from the late 18th century, when Sally Lunn became famous for her home-made tea biscuits which she sold in the streets of Bath.

Method

Warm and grease the tins.

Heat the milk in a pan, dissolve the butter in it and allow mixture to cool until tepid. Sift the warmed flour and salt in a bowl. Beat the egg and add to the milk. Cream the yeast and sugar together and add to this the milk and egg mixture.

Make a well in the flour and strain in the liquid. Mix to a dough. Turn on to a floured board and knead lightly for a few minutes. Put half of the dough into each warmed tin.

Cover with a cloth and set in a warm place to rise until doubled in bulk (about 30 minutes). Bake in the oven (pre-set at 425°F or Mark 7) for 20-25 minutes. Brush with sweetened milk and put back in oven to dry the glaze.

When baked the Sally Lunn is sliced into three rounds. Each side is toasted, then buttered ; the cake is then reshaped and sliced for serving

Lardy, or flead, cakes

1 lb plain flour
1 teaspoon salt
$\frac{1}{2}$ lb flead, or flare, or lard
cold water

These were made in many country districts and, depending on the county, were called either lardy or flead cakes. They were made from the flead, or flare, of the freshly killed pig. This flead is a 'sheet' of thick white fat, similar to beef suet in texture, and is sold by the butcher. It is also used for rendering down into lard. Lard can also be used for this type of 'cake'. The secret of making these cakes was to beat the dough well during mixing, especially when made with 'flead', and to avoid rolling as much as possible.

Method
Sift flour and salt together. Slice flead (or lard) into thin shavings, taking out any skin, add it to the flour and mix with enough cold water (about $7\frac{1}{2}$ fl oz) to make a firm dough. Turn the dough on to a board or table and beat it thoroughly and hard with the end of the rolling pin, turning it over from time to time. Rest it for about 15 minutes, then repeat the whole process twice more. After the third rest, roll the dough out thinly, about $\frac{1}{4}$-$\frac{1}{2}$ inch, cut it into rounds or triangles and bake, on a floured baking sheet, in a hot oven (pre-set at 400°F or Mark 6) for about 20 minutes, or until well risen and golden-brown. The cakes should be crisp and light to eat.

Parkin

8 oz plain flour
$\frac{1}{2}$ teaspoon salt
$\frac{1}{4}$ oz bicarbonate of soda
1 teaspoon mixed spice
4 oz coarse oatmeal
6 oz soft brown sugar
4 oz butter, or lard
4 oz golden syrup, or black treacle
$\frac{1}{4}$ pint milk

There are many recipes for parkin, coming from both Yorkshire and Lancashire. It is essentially a gingerbread but is made with oatmeal in addition to flour. It is always baked in a shallow tin, such as a roasting tin, kept in the piece and served cut into squares. It should be kept a day or two before eating, wrapped in foil to keep it moist. Parkin may be spread with butter and eaten with cheese. It can be quite a solid cake ; this recipe is for a light and more spongy type.

Method
Grease a small roasting tin and line with greaseproof paper. Set oven at 350°F or Mark 4.

Sift the flour with the salt, bicarbonate of soda and spice and mix thoroughly with the oatmeal and sugar. Melt the fat with the treacle and add to the dry ingredients with the milk. Spread in the prepared tin and bake in the pre-set oven for 50 minutes.

Chelsea buns

10 oz plain flour
pinch of salt
2½ fl oz milk
4 oz butter
½ oz yeast
4 oz caster sugar
2 eggs (beaten)
2 oz currants
pinch of mixed spice

Large square cake tin, or roasting tin

This quantity makes about 12 buns.

Method

Sift the flour with the salt into a mixing bowl. Heat the milk carefully to lukewarm, add half the butter and the yeast; stir until dissolved, then mix in half the sugar and the beaten eggs. Make a well in the centre of the flour, tip in the liquid ingredients and beat thoroughly until smooth and elastic. Place the dough in a greased bowl, turn over once, cover with a damp cloth and put in a warm place to rise until the dough is double in bulk (45-50 minutes).

Knock back the dough with the fist, pulling the sides to the centre and turning it over completely. Let it rise again for 30 minutes.

Turn the dough on to a floured board and roll it out to an oblong. Spread the remaining 2 oz butter over the top two-thirds of the dough and then fold in three. Roll out again to about 18 inches square, sprinkle with 1½ oz sugar, currants and spice and roll up like a swiss roll. Cut the roll into twelve slices, 1½ inches thick, and put them close together on greased roasting tin or cake tin. Cover with a damp cloth and set in a warm place to prove for 15-20 minutes. Sprinkle with remaining ½ oz sugar and bake in the oven (pre-set at 425°F or Mark 7) for about 20 minutes.

Yorkshire oatcakes

8 oz fine oatmeal
1 teaspoon salt
½ teaspoon yeast
¾ pint lukewarm water

Girdle, or large thick iron frying pan

For oatcakes, fine oatmeal and water are the chief ingredients, but a small quantity of yeast is also used. This Yorkshire mixture is more of a batter, and is cooked on a girdle or in a thick iron frying pan. In Skipton, a Yorkshire town famous for oatcakes, this batter was at one time cooked on a hot 'bakestone'. When cooked on one side it was peeled off and, while still damp and flexible, was hung on a wooden rail to dry. When required for eating, it was crisped before the fire.

Method
Mix oatmeal with the salt, dissolve the yeast in the water and stir it into the oatmeal. When smooth, cover and leave to stand for about an hour.

Heat the girdle, or frying pan, rub a piece of fat over it, then pour on a cupful of the batter. Cook on a moderate heat for 4-5 minutes, then turn and cook on the other side. Lift off to cool and cut into farls (three-cornered pieces). Continue until all the batter has been cooked.

Scottish oatcakes

10 oz fine, or medium, oatmeal
½ teaspoon salt
1-2 tablespoons melted lard, or
  bacon fat
about ¼ pint hot water

Method
Set oven at 350°F or Mark 4.

Mix oatmeal and salt ; make a well in the centre, pour in the fat and mix in enough hot water to make a stiffish paste. Turn out on to a floured board or table and roll out as quickly as possible. Using a saucepan lid, mark out into two large rounds, then cut these into farls or, if preferred, stamp out into rounds with a plain cutter. Slide on to a baking sheet and bake in the pre-set moderate oven for approximately 10 minutes. Then cool before storing in a tin. The edges of the oatcakes should curl slightly ; handle with care as they are inclined to be brittle.

1 *Rolling out the Scottish oatcake mixture on a floured board ; this has to be done as quickly as possible so that the mixture does not dry out*
2 *Using a saucepan lid as a guide for marking out mixture into a round before dividing into farls*
3 *Scottish oatcakes are served here with pats of butter ; they can also be eaten with jam or honey, or with savoury snacks and spreads*

Singin' hinnie

12 oz plain flour
good pinch of salt
scant $\frac{1}{2}$ teaspoon bicarbonate of soda
1 teaspoon cream of tartar
3 oz good lard
4 oz currants (well cleaned)
sufficient milk to make a fairly soft
    dough (about $7\frac{1}{2}$ fl oz)

Girdle, or thick iron frying pan

This is a North Country girdle cake. It gets its name from the fact that it 'sings' (sizzles) as it cooks on the girdle.

Method
Sift the flour, salt, bicarbonate of soda and cream of tartar together. Rub in the fat and then add the currants. Mix to a dough with milk and turn out on to a floured board ; pat or roll out into a round about $\frac{1}{4}$ inch thick. Heat a girdle or thick iron frying pan ; flour lightly then pat the 'hinnie' on to it. Cook on gentle heat for about 5 minutes, then turn and cook on the other side for the same time (both sides should be nicely brown). Then take off, cool slightly, split and butter. Serve hot, as a teacake.

Above : cooking singin' hinnie on girdle before turning it over to cook until brown on the other side
Below : buttering the cooked singin' hinnie after it has been split

Banbury cakes

8 oz flaky pastry (well chilled) — see right

For filling
2 oz butter
1 tablespoon plain flour
4 oz currants
2 tablespoons mixed peel (finely chopped)
$\frac{1}{2}$ teaspoon ground allspice, or grated nutmeg
4 dessertspoons caster sugar
1 tablespoon rum (optional)
1 egg white (beaten)
caster sugar (for dusting)

Method

Melt the butter, blend in the flour and cook gently for 2 minutes. Add the well-washed currants, the peel, spice or grated nutmeg, sugar and rum, if used, and simmer for 2-3 minutes. Allow to cool.

Set oven at 425°F or Mark 7. Roll out the pastry $\frac{1}{8}$ inch thick, turn it over and cut large rounds about the size of a saucer, damp top edges and put a good tablespoon of prepared filling on each. Draw the edges into the centre and seal them together ; turn the cakes over and roll each round to an oblong, pinching each end to a point to give the traditional Banbury cake shape.

Make three slashes on the top, place the cakes on a baking sheet and bake in the pre-set oven for 15 minutes. Then brush them with beaten egg, dust them with the caster sugar and continue cooking for 5 minutes longer. Dust again with sugar before serving.

Flaky pastry

8 oz plain flour
pinch of salt
3 oz butter
3 oz lard
$\frac{1}{4}$ pint ice-cold water (to mix)

Method

Sift the flour with salt into a bowl. Divide the fats into four portions (two of butter, two of lard) ; rub one portion — either lard or butter — into the flour and mix to a firm dough with cold water. The amount of water varies with different flour but an average quantity for 8 oz flour is 4-5 fl oz (about $\frac{1}{4}$ pint or 8-10 tablespoons) ; the finer the flour the more water it will absorb.

Knead the dough lightly until smooth, then roll out to an oblong. Put a second portion of fat (not the same kind as first portion rubbed in) in small pieces on to two-thirds of the dough. Fold in three, half turn the dough to bring the open edge towards you and roll out again to an oblong. Put on a third portion of fat in pieces, fold dough in three, wrap in a cloth or polythene bag and leave in a cool place for 15 minutes.

Roll out dough again, put on remaining fat in pieces, fold and roll as before. If pastry looks at all streaky, give one more turn and roll again.

Cloutie dumpling

12 oz self-raising flour
6 oz suet (chopped or shredded)
4 oz each of currants, sultanas and
stoned raisins (cleaned and mixed)
½ apple (grated)
1 rounded teaspoon each of
cinnamon, ground ginger and
mixed spice
5 oz soft brown sugar
½ teaspoon each of bicarbonate
of soda and cream of tartar
1 egg (beaten)
3 tablespoons treacle
about ¼ pint milk (to mix)

This is a pudding boiled in a cloth. In some parts of Scotland it is made for a special occasion, such as a birthday, and for Hallowe'en, when charms are put in it, as in an English Christmas pudding.

Hard sauce

For a brandy butter, take 4 oz unsalted butter, 4 oz caster sugar and 2-3 table-spoons brandy.

For rum butter, take 3 oz unsalted butter, 3 oz soft brown sugar, grated rind of ½ lemon and squeeze of juice, and 2-3 tablespoons rum.

Cream butter thoroughly, gradually beat in sugar (and add lemon rind and juice for rum butter) ; continue beating until white, then add brandy (or rum), a teaspoon at a time, to flavour butter well. Work in a little chopped glacé ginger if liked. Pile up in a small dish and chill well before serving.

Method

Mix the flour, suet, dried fruit and apple, spices, sugar and raising agents together. Mix the treacle with the egg and add this to the mixture with just enough milk to make a soft dough, like a scone dough. Turn into a scalded, floured cloth and tie up, leaving room for the dumpling to swell.

Have ready a large pan full of boiling water, plunge in the dumpling and give it three hours of steady boiling. Replenish with boiling water as it evaporates. Turn pudding out on to a hot dish, removing cloth, and put it in the oven (at 350°F or Mark 4) for 10 minutes. This will dry it off and glaze the top.

Serve with sugar, or a custard, or hard sauce. Any dumpling left over is cut into slices and fried with bacon for breakfast or high tea.

Above : wrapping cloutie dumpling in a scalded, floured cloth which is then tied to leave room for the dumpling to swell while cooking Right : cloutie dumpling is sliced and served with sugar, custard, or a brandy or rum butter (hard sauce)

Speckled bread from Anglesey

12 oz mixed fruit, 8 oz sugar
(brown or white), 1 cup hot tea
(soaked together overnight)
2 oz butter
1 lb self-raising flour
pinch of salt
1 egg (well beaten)

2 lb loaf tin

This bread is very easy to make and keeps well.

Method
Grease the loaf tin and set oven at 350°F or Mark 4. Rub the butter and flour together, with salt, then add the egg. Add the soaked ingredients and mix well together. Put mixture in greased tin and bake in the pre-set moderate oven for $1\frac{1}{2}$-$1\frac{3}{4}$ hours, or a little less.

Shortbread

6 oz unsalted butter
$3\frac{1}{2}$ oz caster sugar
6 oz plain flour
3 oz rice flour, or fine semolina

For decoration
mixed candied peel
almonds (blanched and split) —
see page 154

9-inch diameter flan ring, or sandwich tin

Method
Set oven at 375°F or Mark 5. Cream butter in a bowl and gradually work in 3 oz of the caster sugar. Then mix in the flours (sifted together) as quickly as possible to make a paste. Press into a flan ring set on a baking sheet, or in a sandwich tin. Shortbread should be $\frac{3}{4}$-1 inch thick.

Mark into slices with the back of a knife and decorate with pieces of candied peel and blanched, split almonds. The candied peel may be chopped and worked into the paste, and the top decorated with the almonds. Dust with remaining caster sugar and cook for 15-20 minutes in the pre-set oven.

Cool shortbread before removing from the tin.

Selkirk bannock

1½ lb plain flour
½ teaspoon salt
4 oz butter, or lard
8 oz sultanas
4 oz currants
2 oz candied peel (finely chopped)
3 oz caster sugar
½ oz yeast
½-¾ pint warm milk
plain flour (for dusting)
2 tablespoons milk, mixed with 1
    tablespoon caster sugar (for
    glazing)

This is a bun loaf, baked in one large round about the size of a dinner plate and 2-3 inches deep. It is moderately rich in fruit and is cut across in ¼-inch slices, buttered and eaten for tea or with cheese for lunch.

Method

Sift flour with salt into a warm bowl. Rub in the fat, add the cleaned fruit, peel and caster sugar, leaving 1 teaspoon of sugar to cream with the yeast.

Cream yeast in a bowl with remaining sugar. Add milk, and then yeast liquid, to the dry ingredients. Mix to a fairly firm dough, then turn out on to a board and knead well for about 5 minutes.

Put mixture into a large bowl, dust with flour and cover with a damp cloth. Leave in a warm place for 1-1½ hours to rise until doubled in bulk. Remove dough from bowl and knead lightly to shape it into a large round. Set on a floured baking sheet and leave to prove again for about 20 minutes. Meanwhile set oven at 400°F or Mark 6.

Bake for about 1 hour in preset oven ; after 50 minutes glaze top by brushing with sweetened milk. Lower heat slightly to 375°F or Mark 5 and bake for a further 30 minutes, or until cooked. When cooked, it should be brown and if turned upside down should sound hollow when bottom is tapped.

Haman taschen (Haman's pockets)

8 oz plain flour
½ oz yeast
1 oz caster sugar
¼ pint milk
1 oz butter
pinch of salt
1 egg (beaten)
melted butter (for brushing)
filling of choice (see right)
honey, or beaten egg (for brushing)

Method

Cream the yeast with 1 teaspoon of the measured sugar. Heat the milk until it is lukewarm, then melt the butter in it and pour this on to the yeast.

Sift the flour and salt into a warm mixing bowl. Make a well in the centre, pour in the yeast mixture and mix to a dough. Cover the bowl with a damp cloth and leave dough in a warm place to rise until it is doubled in bulk. Then add remaining sugar and beaten egg and knead well. Set dough aside, covered, to rise again.

Roll out dough on a floured board to ¼-inch thickness. Cut out 4-inch rounds and brush each one with melted butter. Place a spoonful of the chosen filling in the centre of each round. Pull the edges in and form a tricorn shape, with some filling showing. Place tricorns on a baking sheet, then leave in a warm place to prove. Set the oven at 350°F or Mark 4. Brush the Haman taschen with honey (or beaten egg) and bake in the pre-set oven for 20 minutes until golden-brown.

Below : folding the circles of Haman taschen dough into tricorn shapes, with some of the filling showing
Right : a plateful of Haman taschen, three-cornered pockets with a sweet poppy seed filling, which are eaten at the Jewish festival of Esther

Fillings

Warm 1 tablespoon honey and ½ oz butter together. Add to them 1 teaspoon lemon juice, 1 oz ground almonds and 4 oz ground poppyseeds, or cooked prunes, or chopped sultanas or raisins. Allow to cool before using.

Hot cross buns

1 lb plain flour
½ teaspoon salt
½ teaspoon mixed spice
scant ½ pint milk
¾ oz yeast (fresh, or dried)
2-4 oz butter
2 oz caster sugar
2 eggs (beaten)
6 oz currants (cleaned)
1 oz candied peel (finely
    chopped) — optional
little extra plain flour (for dusting)
sweetened milk (for finishing)

Nowadays these buns are made individually but they were originally baked as one large bun. This quantity makes about 16 buns.

Method

Sift the flour with salt and mixed spice into a bowl. Warm the milk carefully to blood heat (98°F) and add the yeast and butter. Stir until yeast is dissolved, then mix in the sugar and eggs. Make a well in the flour, tip in the liquid ingredients and beat until smooth.

Turn dough on to a floured board, work in the currants and candied peel. Knead dough until it is elastic, then place it in a warmed, greased bowl. Sprinkle the dough with extra flour and cover with a clean tea towel.

Set dough to rise in a warm place for 1½ hours, or until it is doubled in bulk, then knock down dough and leave to rise again for another 30 minutes. Set oven at 425°F or Mark 7.

Shape the dough into small, round buns; with the back of a knife, mark each one with a cross on the top. Arrange the buns on a greased baking sheet and leave to prove until they are nearly twice their size (about 15 minutes).
Note : strips of shortcrust pastry or a special flour and water paste may be used to make the crosses.

Brush bun tops with a little sweetened milk and bake them in pre-set oven for 15 minutes.

A steamy atmosphere in the oven is best for baking buns; this can be obtained by placing a roasting tin of boiling water at the bottom of the oven.

Leave buns to cool; when cold put them in a polythene bag and store in the bread bin.

Coffee breads and pastries

Coffee breads are so called because they are often served with coffee on the Continent. For very special occasions they sometimes appear at breakfast-time, but they are also suitable for tea-time and, eaten with curd cheese or butter, they make an excellent lunchtime alternative to a pudding.

The doughs in this chapter may be divided into three sections : for coffee breads, a rich dough including eggs, milk, yeast and butter ; for brioches, a dough using the same ingredients as coffee breads but with a completely different method of introducing the yeast ; for Danish pastries and French croissants, where yeast is added to a flour and water dough and then butter rolled in as for flaky, or puff, pastry. Many of these doughs or pastes have a high proportion of yeast which, with the butter and eggs, gives a rich spongy texture and a soft crust.

When trying out these recipes for the first time, it is wise to start with the less rich doughs because you do need more skill to make the very rich ones.

Foundation dough for 'coffee' breads

1 lb plain flour
large pinch of salt
7 fl oz milk
1 oz yeast
4 oz butter
4 oz caster sugar
2 eggs (beaten)

Method
Sift the flour with the salt into a mixing bowl. Warm the milk carefully to blood heat, add to yeast and butter, stir until dissolved and then mix in the sugar and beaten eggs. Make a well in the centre of the flour, pour in the liquid ingredients and mix until smooth, first with a wooden spoon and then with your hand. When the dough comes away cleanly from the sides of the bowl, turn it on to a floured board and knead until it becomes elastic.

Place the dough in a greased bowl (turn it in the bowl so that it is lightly greased all over), cover with a damp cloth and set dough to rise in a warm place for 45-50 minutes or until it has doubled in bulk. Knock down the dough, pull the sides to the centre, turn it over, cover and let it rise again for 30 minutes before shaping and baking.

Honey twist

1 lb quantity of foundation dough (see left)

For topping
2 oz butter (melted)
6 tablespoons clear honey
2 oz caster sugar
1 oz plain flour
1½ oz almonds (blanched and chopped) — see page 154

Shallow 10-inch diameter cake tin (about 2½ inches deep)

Method
Well grease the cake tin. Turn the dough on to a floured board and shape into a long narrow roll, about 1-inch thick. Coil the roll into the prepared tin, beginning at the outside edge and twisting as you go. Leave a little space between the coils. Cover the tin with a damp cloth and allow dough to rise in a warm place for 35-40 minutes until the mixture comes to the top of the tin or until it is well risen.

Set oven at 400°F or Mark 6.

Mix all the ingredients for the topping together and spoon over the bread. Bake for about 35-45 minutes in pre-set oven.

French fruit braid

1 lb quantity of foundation
  dough (see page 51)

For filling
1 large cooking apple (about 1 lb,
  or just over)
½ lb raisins (seeded)
4 oz brown sugar
½ teaspoon cinnamon
1 oz butter

For icing
6 tablespoons icing sugar (mixed
  with 1 tablespoon water)

Method
To prepare the filling : while
dough is rising for the second
time, peel and core the apple,
chop it roughly and put in a
pan with the other ingredients.
Cook until apple is soft and
pulpy, then allow it to cool.

Turn the dough on to a
floured board, roll out to an
oblong about 8 inches by 14
inches. Spread the fruit mixture
down the middle, covering a
space about 3 inches wide. At
each side of the filling make
cuts 2 inches long at 1-inch
intervals. Take a strip from each
side and cross to form a plait.
Tuck the last two strips underneath end of the braid.

Lift the plait on to a well-
greased baking sheet, cover with
a damp cloth, leave it to rise in
a warm place for about 30
minutes until it has doubled its
size.

Bake in oven (pre-set at 400°F
or Mark 6) for 35-40 minutes.
While still warm, brush braid
with icing.

*Spreading the filling for the French
fruit braid down the centre of the
rolled-out dough. Then cutting the
dough diagonally on each side of
filling so that the strips can be
plaited to give the braided effect*

The dough at the end of the oblong is folded and the strips are plaited over the filling. The last two strips are then folded underneath

French fruit braid is popular for morning coffee parties

Easter tea ring

½ lb quantity of foundation dough
(see page 51)
1 oz butter (softened)
2 oz caster sugar
2 oz raisins
1 teaspoon ground cinnamon
(optional)

For decoration
soft icing (as for stollen, see page
56)
about 1 oz walnut kernels
1 oz glacé cherries
1 oz angelica

If making this tea ring for a
party, double the quantities and
it will then be sufficient to serve
8-10 people.

Method

Have the foundation dough
ready after the second rising.
Turn on to a floured board and
roll out to an oblong approximately 9 inches by 6 inches.
The dough should be $\frac{1}{4}$-$\frac{1}{2}$ inch
thick. Cover surface with pats
of butter, sprinkle with sugar,
raisins and cinnamon. Then
roll up the dough tightly, beginning at the wide side, and seal
by pinching the edges well
together. Curl the dough round
into a ring, joining the ends
together well, and place on a
greased baking tin. Snip the
ring at 1-inch intervals with
scissors, making each cut or
snip two-thirds through the
ring. Cover with a cloth and
prove for about 15-20 minutes.
   Bake until golden-brown in
a hot oven, pre-set at 400°F or
Mark 6, for about 25 minutes.
Pierce the roll with a thin skewer
at the end of this time to test if
the ring is done. Mix the icing
and brush this over the tea ring
while still warm. Decorate with
the nuts, cherries and angelica
and then lightly brush again
with icing.

*Below : rolling up dough covered
with the butter, sugar, raisins and
cinnamon for Easter tea ring*
*Below right : snipping the dough after
it has been rolled up and made into
a ring before the final proving*

Decorating the cooked tea ring ; the icing should be spread on while the ring is still warm from the oven

Easter tea ring, decorated with icing, walnuts, glacé cherries and angelica

Stollen

½ lb quantity of foundation dough
   (see page 51)
1½ oz almonds
1 oz glacé cherries
about ¾ oz citron peel
1½ oz seeded raisins
1½ oz sultanas
grated rind of ½ lemon
1½ oz butter
soft, or glacé, icing (made with 3
   tablespoons icing sugar mixed
   with 1-2 tablespoons syrup, or
   water), or icing sugar

Method

Blanch and chop the almonds,
quarter the cherries, shred the
peel and mix it with the raisins,
sultanas and lemon rind. After
the dough has risen twice, turn it
on to a floured board and knead
in the fruit, pat or roll it out to
an oval about 8 inches by 10
inches and spread with about
1 oz softened butter. Fold in
two lengthwise and shape into
a crescent. Press in the double
edges firmly together.

Place the stollen on a greased
baking sheet, melt the remaining butter and brush the top of
the stollen with it. Prove dough
in a warm place for about 30
minutes. Bake in a moderately
hot oven, pre-set at 400°F or
Mark 6, for 30-35 minutes.

Make the icing and while the
stollen is still warm pour it over
the top. Or simply dredge the
stollen with icing sugar.

Streusel kuchen

1 lb quantity of foundation dough
   (see page 51)

For streusel
2½ oz brown sugar
¾ oz plain flour
1 teaspoon cinnamon
1 oz butter (melted)
2 oz walnuts (chopped)

2 lb cake, or loaf, tin

Method

Grease the tin well. Set the oven
at 400°F or Mark 6. After the
second rising divide the dough
in two. Put half into the prepared tin and push it down with
your fist. Mix the ingredients
for the streusel together, put
half of this on top of the dough,
then cover with the other half
of the dough, and scatter the
rest of the streusel mixture over
the top.

Prove for 10-15 minutes, then
bake for about 45-50 minutes.
Test with a thin skewer before
taking it out of the oven.

Apple streusel kuchen

$\frac{1}{2}$ lb quantity of foundation dough
   (see page 51)

For apple mixture
1-1$\frac{1}{2}$ lb dessert apples
   (preferably Laxton)
1-2 oz butter (melted)
streusel (as for streusel kuchen —
   see left)

*Deep 7-inch diameter sandwich tin,
or spring-form mould*

It is important that the apples should not be too watery, ie. cooking apples such as Bramley are not suitable for this. Use dessert apples, such as Laxton, which have a sub-acid content.

Method
Have the dough ready after second rising, knead the dough lightly and press on to the bottom of sandwich tin or mould. Set aside. Peel, core and quarter the apples, cut each quarter in half lengthwise then sauté quickly in the butter for about 3-4 minutes, turning them frequently with a slice. Draw aside, cool and then spoon the apple slices on top of the dough.

Prepare the streusel by mixing the ingredients together, scatter over the top of the apple and dough and prove for about 10-15 minutes. Then bake in a hot oven, pre-set at 400°F or Mark 6, for about 45 minutes. If the streusel browns too quickly, lower the heat to 375°F or Mark 5 and cook for the same length of time. Take out and cool slightly before serving. This may alternatively be served warm as a pudding.

Nut bread

6$\frac{1}{4}$ oz plain flour
pinch of salt
4 oz butter
$\frac{3}{4}$ oz yeast
1 oz caster sugar
about 5 tablespoons tepid milk
   and water (mixed)
extra caster sugar (to decorate)

For filling
3$\frac{1}{2}$ oz hazelnuts (browned and
   ground)
4 oz caster sugar
2 oz cake crumbs
1 small egg (mixed with 1 tablespoon water)

1 lb loaf tin

Method
Lightly grease the loaf tin. Sieve flour and salt into a warm basin and rub in 3 oz butter. Cream the yeast with 1 teaspoon of the sugar and add the rest of the sugar to the flour. Pour the tepid milk and water on to the yeast and mix into the flour. Knead well to a fairly firm dough and put into a buttered bowl ; cover with a damp cloth and leave in a warm place for about 45 minutes until it has risen.

Mix all the ingredients for the filling together. Roll the dough the width of the ready-greased tin and about 20 inches long. Spread with the filling and roll up from each end towards the centre. Put into the prepared tin and prove for 15 minutes.

Bake in a pre-set oven at 400°F or Mark 6 for 8-10 minutes, then lower the heat to 325°F or Mark 3, and continue cooking for about 1 hour. Remove from the tin and cool, brush with the remaining ounce of butter (melted) and sprinkle with caster sugar.

Gannat

½ lb plain flour (sifted with 2
    pinches of salt and 1 of pepper)
1 teaspoon caster sugar
½ oz yeast
4 fl oz milk
2 oz butter, or luxury margarine
2 eggs
4 oz Gruyère, or Emmenthal, or
    Cheshire, cheese (grated)

*Deep 7-inch diameter sandwich tin,
or 1 lb loaf tin*

This is a rich cheese bread
which makes delicious sandwiches or can be used as a
bread and butter accompani-
ment to a first course.

Method
Place flour in a warm bowl and
make a well in the centre.
Cream sugar with yeast and
place in the well of flour.
    Warm milk with butter in a
pan ; when dissolved and the
mixture is only lukewarm, stir
into the flour with the eggs, well
beaten to a froth.
    Work well to form a soft
dough, cover and leave to stand
until double in bulk (45 minutes
to 1 hour). Then work in the
cheese, reserving 1 tablespoon.
    Set oven at 400°F or Mark 6.
    Turn mixture into the greased
tin. Leave to prove, sprinkle with
rest of cheese and bake in pre-
set oven for about 45-50
minutes, until a good brown.
Serve hot or cold.
    If baked in a sandwich tin, it
may be split and sandwiched
with cheese cream.

Kugelhopf

about 7 fl oz milk
scant 1 oz yeast
12 oz plain flour
pinch of salt
1 oz caster sugar
2 large, or 3 small, eggs (well
    broken with a fork)
4 oz butter (melted)
2 oz currants (washed and dried)
2 oz raisins, or sultanas (washed
    and dried)
about 24 almonds (blanched) — see
    page 154
icing sugar (optional)

7-8 inch diameter kugelhopf tin

Method
Butter the tin well. Warm the
milk to blood heat, pour on to
the yeast and stir until dissolved. Sift the flour and salt into
a warm bowl, make a well in the
centre, pour in the warm milk
and yeast, add the sugar and
eggs and the melted (but not
hot) butter. Mix thoroughly

*Turning the kugelhopf dough, mixed
with dried fruit, into kugelhopf tin*

together, then add the cleaned, dried fruit. Press the blanched almonds round the sides and bottom of the buttered tin. Turn the dough into it so that it is three-quarters full, then stand it in a warm place for about 20-30 minutes, or until the mixture is about 1 inch below the top of the tin.

Meanwhile set the oven at 375-400°F or Mark 5-6. Stand the tin on a thick baking sheet, then put into the centre of the pre-set oven and bake for 50-60 minutes. If the top tends to colour too much, lower the heat until the kugelhopf is done. Leave for a few minutes before turning out and dust with icing sugar if wanted.

A kugelhopf is generally eaten with coffee, but not tea. It is baked in a special fluted tin with a tube in the centre, known as a kugelhopf tin

Brioches

8 oz plain flour
scant $\frac{1}{2}$ oz yeast
2-3 tablespoons tepid water
1 tablespoon caster sugar
1 teaspoon salt
2 eggs
about 2-4 tablespoons milk (if
  necessary)
4 oz butter
extra plain flour (for sprinkling)
1 egg (beaten) — mixed with 1
  tablespoon milk and a large pinch
  of salt (for brushing)

8-9 fluted brioche tins

Brioche dough is rich, light-textured and has a soft brown crust when cooked. The dough can vary in richness according to the proportion of eggs and butter. The richer kind of dough makes the well known brioches, a plainer dough can be used for brioche buns.

Method
Sift the flour ; dissolve yeast in water and mix it well with about a quarter of the flour to make a small ball of dough. Cut a cross on top of the dough to encourage it to rise, and drop it into a large bowl of hand-hot water. When the ball is nearly double in size and has risen to the surface it is ready to mix with the other ingredients.

Meanwhile, make a well in the remaining flour and place the sugar, salt and eggs in it ; mix together to a slack dough, using 2-4 tablespoons of milk if necessary. Beat the dough until it is elastic in texture and looks like chamois leather.

Cream the butter until soft and work it into the dough ; then drain the yeast ball and cut and fold it into the mixture very carefully. Knead the dough into a large ball, place it in a greased bowl, sprinkle with flour, cover with a cloth and leave to rise at room temperature, for $1\frac{1}{2}$-2 hours. When the dough has doubled its bulk knock it down, pull the sides to the centre and turn it over. Sprinkle again with flour, cover with a cloth and put in a cool larder or refrigerator overnight or for 6-7 hours.

The next day grease the tins, and divide the dough into 8-9 even-size pieces. Knead and

Placing yeast and flour dough in a bowl of hand-hot water

Cutting yeast cake into butter, flour and egg mixture

shape them with the hand,
place in brioche tins, or half
fill the brioche tins, cut a cross
on the top and crown with a
small ball or 'head' of dough.

Let the brioches rise in a warm
place for 15-20 minutes, then
brush carefully with beaten egg.
Bake in oven, pre-set at 425°F
or Mark 7, for 15-20 minutes.

Left : putting dough in brioche tins
Below : serve hot brioches, with
butter, for breakfast continental style

Brioche buns

12 oz plain flour
pinch of salt
scant 1 oz yeast
2 oz caster sugar
2 eggs
2-3 tablespoons milk (if necessary)
2-4 oz butter (creamed)
apricot, or other, jam (to taste)

To finish
soft icing (see stollen, page 56), or
thin apricot glaze, or 1 rounded
tablespoon caster sugar and 1
tablespoon milk (warmed and
mixed together)

This quantity makes 12-16 buns.

Method
Sift the flour with salt on to your work surface, divide into four crosswise using the edge of the hand. Draw one quarter aside, make a well in the centre of this and crumble in the yeast. Have ready a basin or pan of hand-hot water, put 1-2 tablespoons of this on to the yeast mixture and mix up to a soft dough, adding a little more water if necessary. Make a cross-cut on the top of this yeast cake with scissors and then drop it into the warm water.

Add the sugar to the remaining flour, break in the eggs and beat up to a soft elastic dough, adding as much of the milk as necessary. Beat thoroughly until very elastic. This can be done in a basin, on a table, or in a mixer with a paddle or dough hook.

By this time the yeast cake will have risen to the surface of the water. Add the creamed butter to the dough and when mixed (no beating is necessary here) lift the yeast cake out of the water and stir into the mixture. Put into a floured basin, cover and put in the refrigerator overnight, or for 3-4 hours. At the end of this time the dough will be well risen. If leaving overnight, it may be necessary to push the dough down when it has risen to the top of the basin. By leaving it to rise in this way the dough is firm and easy to handle.

To shape into buns, lift out, put on to a lightly floured board or table and then roll out, spread with the jam and roll up like a swiss roll. Press edges together and cut into slices about $\frac{3}{4}$ inch thick. Lay these, cut side down, on a well-greased baking sheet. Cover with a cloth and leave to prove for 8-10 minutes.

Bake in a hot oven pre-set at 400°F or Mark 6, for 10-15 minutes. Then take out, cool slightly and brush with the soft icing. Alternatively, brush with a little milk glaze or thin apricot glaze and put back into the oven for 2-3 minutes. Take out and cool.

Brioche loaf

Use the brioche recipe on page 60, but increase the butter from 4 oz to 6 oz. After leaving the dough overnight, knead it and place in a loaf tin $8\frac{1}{2}$ inches by $4\frac{1}{2}$ inches by $2\frac{1}{2}$ inches deep. Prove in a warm place for about 20 minutes and then arrange sliced, candied fruits over the top. Bake in a hot oven, pre-set at 400°F or Mark 6, for 45-60 minutes. While warm, brush with soft icing (see stollen, page 56).

French croissants

8 oz plain flour
¼ oz yeast
2-3 tablespoons tepid water
½ teaspoon salt
1 tablespoon caster sugar
4 oz butter
about 3 tablespoons milk
1 egg (beaten) — for brushing

This quantity makes 18 croissants.

Method

Sift the flour. Dissolve the yeast in the water and mix with a quarter of the flour to make a small ball of dough. Cut a cross on top and drop this yeast cake into a large bowl of warm water.

Meanwhile mix the remaining flour with the salt, sugar, half the butter and sufficient milk to give a soft, but not slack, dough. The dough for croissants should not be as soft as for brioches. Beat the dough on the pastry board until it is smooth and elastic. When the yeast cake has risen to the surface of the water and is almost double its size, drain carefully and mix into the dough thoroughly. Put the dough into a floured bowl, cover and leave overnight in a cool larder or refrigerator.

Shape the remaining butter into a flat cake. Turn the dough on to a floured board, roll it out to an oblong and place the butter in the centre. Fold one third of the dough over the butter and fold the other third of the dough on top to make 3 layers. Turn the folded dough so that one of the open ends faces front. Roll out again, fold over as before and turn. Repeat once more. Wrap in a cloth and leave for 15 minutes in a cool place. Repeat the rolling and folding twice more.

To shape the croissants : roll the dough to an oblong, ⅛ inch thick, divide lengthways and cut each strip into triangles. Roll up, starting from the base, curl and place on a lightly floured baking sheet. Cover with a cloth and prove in a warm place for 15-20 minutes. Brush with beaten egg and bake in a hot oven, pre-set at 425°F or Mark 7, for 5 minutes, then reduce the heat to 375°F or Mark 5 and continue cooking for about 10 minutes, until the croissants are browned.

Danish pastries (basic recipe)

12 oz plain flour
large pinch of salt
1 oz yeast
2 oz caster sugar
1 teacup lukewarm milk
9 oz butter
1 egg (beaten)
little extra egg (beaten) — for
   brushing
soft icing (see stollen, page 56)

This quantity will make 12
pastries of any shape.

Method

Sift the flour with the salt into
a mixing bowl. Cream the yeast
with the sugar until liquid, add a
good teacup of lukewarm milk
and 2 oz of the butter, stir until
dissolved ; then add the beaten
egg. Pour these liquid ingredients into the flour and mix to a
smooth dough. Cover the dough
and leave at room temperature
for about 1 hour or until double
in bulk. Punch down the dough,
turn it on to a floured board and
knead lightly. Roll out to an
oblong and cover two-thirds
of the dough with half the
remaining butter, divided in
small pieces. Fold dough in
three, unbuttered portion first,
half turn to bring open edge
towards you and roll out again
to an oblong. Fold in three and
roll again. Put on the remaining
butter, cut into pieces, fold and
leave for 15 minutes. Roll and
fold twice more and leave again
for 15 minutes. Chill the dough
for a little while.

Roll pastry to $\frac{1}{2}$ inch thick, shape
as required. Prove, brush with
beaten egg and bake in oven,
pre-set at 400°F or Mark 6, for
25 minutes. Ice pastries while
warm.

*Dotting two-thirds of Danish pastry
dough with pieces of butter*

*Folding dough into three, with the
unbuttered portion on the inside*

*Half turn the folded dough round on
the board and then roll it again*

Shapes for Danish pastries

Cartwheels

Roll out the Danish pastry dough as thinly as possible to a large oblong, spread carefully with a very thin layer of almond filling, then sprinkle with raisins and roll it up as for a swiss roll. Cut the roll into $\frac{1}{4}$-inch slices, and place the slices, cut side down, on a greased baking tin. Prove, brush with beaten egg and sprinkle flaked almonds on the top before baking.

Crescents

Roll dough into a large circle $\frac{1}{8}$ inch thick and cut it into triangles or wedges. Pour a little almond filling on each triangle and roll them up loosely, starting at the base of the triangle, and then shape into crescents. Prove and bake.

A selection of Danish pastries : top, left to right : cartwheels, envelope, comb ; centre ; pinwheels ; bottom : crescents

Shapes for Danish pastries continued

Pinwheels

Roll out dough thinly and cut it into 4-inch squares. Cut the dough from each corner to within a $\frac{1}{2}$ inch of the centre. Put a little jam or almond filling in the centre, then fold four alternate points to the centre, pressing them down firmly. Prove and bake.

Shaping the dough into pinwheels

Envelopes

Roll out the dough thinly and cut into 4-inch squares. Spread with vanilla cream and fold the corners in towards the middle. Press the edges down lightly. Prove, then bake for 12-15 minutes.

Combs

Roll out the dough fairly thinly and cut into strips about 5 inches wide. Place an apple or almond filling in the middle and fold both sides over. Brush lightly with beaten egg and roll in crushed loaf sugar and chopped almonds. Cut into pieces about 4 inches long and gash about four or five times on one side ; open out the slits slightly. Prove, then bake for 12-15 minutes. These combs can be brushed slightly with beaten egg before baking to give them a glazed finish.

Fillings
Vanilla cream

1 tablespoon plain flour
1 teaspoon cornflour
1 egg yolk
1 tablespoon caster sugar
$\frac{1}{4}$ pint milk
2-3 drops of vanilla essence

Method
Work the flours, egg yolk and sugar together, adding a little milk. Bring the rest of the milk to the boil, pour on to the mixture, blend and return to the pan. Stir until boiling. Allow to cool then flavour with a few drops of vanilla essence.

Almond filling

2 oz almonds (ground)
2 oz caster sugar
little beaten egg

Method
Mix the almonds and sugar together and bind with enough egg to bring to a firm paste.

Apple filling

1 lb cooking apples
$\frac{1}{2}$ oz butter
grated rind and juice of $\frac{1}{2}$ lemon
3-4 tablespoons granulated sugar

This can be used for any shape of Danish pastries and the pastries can either be finished with a soft icing or brushed with a little apricot glaze (see page 152).

Method
Wipe the apples, quarter and core them, but do not peel. Rub the butter round a saucepan, slice in the apples and add the grated rind and lemon juice. Cover and cook them slowly to a pulp.

Rub pulp through a nylon strainer, return to the rinsed-out pan with the sugar. Cook gently until thick. Turn out and allow to get quite cold before using. This can be turned into a jam jar and used as required.

Grapfruit

8 oz quantity of brioche dough (see brioches, page 60)
blackcurrant, or strawberry, conserve or other whole fruit jam
deep fat
caster sugar

2 $\frac{1}{2}$ - inch diameter cutter

Grapfruit are similar to rich doughnuts.

Method
Have the brioche dough ready, make sure that it is quite firm. Roll it out to about $\frac{1}{2}$ -inch thickness, and with a round cutter stamp out in rounds. Put a teaspoon of the fruit from the jam in the centre of each one, brush round the edges with a little water, then shape into balls. Leave these balls in a warm place for about 5 minutes or until they are only just beginning to rise. Heat the fat to about 360-370°F and drop in the grapfruit. Fry for about 7-8 minutes, slowly increasing the heat. Turn them occasionally as they swell and brown. Then lift out, drain them well and roll in caster sugar.

Coffee bread with toppings

6 oz plain flour
good pinch of salt
2 teaspoons baking powder
2 oz shortening, or lard
6 oz granulated sugar
1 egg (beaten)
4 fl oz milk

$8\frac{1}{2}$ - 9 inch diameter, or square, cake tin

Method
Grease and flour tin and set the oven at 375°F or Mark 5.

Sift the flour, salt and baking powder into a mixing bowl. Rub in the fat, add the sugar and make a well in the centre. Mix the beaten egg with the milk and pour into the well in the flour mixture; stir until a thick batter is formed, then beat thoroughly for 4-5 minutes. (This will have the effect of thickening the batter.)

Turn mixture into prepared tin and cover with chosen topping (see following recipes). Bake in pre-set oven for about 30 minutes.

If baking in a square tin, serve cut into squares; if a round tin is used, cut in thin slices. This is better eaten warm, and goes well with coffee.

1 *Pouring batter for coffee bread into greased and floured tin*
2 *Sprinkling cinnamon topping over coffee bread mixture*

Marmalade topping

scant 3 oz plain flour
3 oz soft brown sugar
2 tablespoons melted butter
1 tablespoon single cream, or
   top of milk
3 tablespoons marmalade

Method
Mix all ingredients together and turn on top of the raw cake mixture.

Cinnamon topping

1½ oz walnut kernels
3 oz soft brown sugar
2 teaspoons cinnamon

Method

Coarsely chop the walnut kernels and scatter them over the raw cake mixture. Mix the sugar and cinnamon together and sprinkle on top.

Apple topping

1 large cooking apple
1 rounded teaspoon cinnamon
3 tablespoons caster sugar

Method

Peel and slice the apple and stick into the surface of the raw cake mixture. Mix the cinnamon and sugar together and dust it over the top.

Left : coffee bread with cinnamon topping. Right : date bread (see page 70)

Coffee buns

12 oz self-raising flour
pinch of salt
3 oz shortening
5 oz soft brown sugar
1 egg
about 1 tablespoon strong
  coffee essence (to flavour)
scant $\frac{1}{4}$ pint milk
coffee glacé, or butter, icing, or
  coffee butter cream (see pages
  97 and 152)

This quantity makes about 14 buns. They must be made on the day they are to be eaten.

Method
Grease 2 baking sheets and set the oven at 425°F or Mark 7.

Sift the flour with the salt into a mixing bowl, add the fat and rub it in finely, then stir in the sugar. Beat the egg with the coffee essence and add enough milk to give $\frac{1}{4}$ pint of liquid in all. Add this mixture to the flour, fat and sugar and mix with a wooden spoon until smooth.

Divide the dough into 14 even-size pieces, mould these in the hand into rounds, or ovals, place them on the greased sheets and bake for about 15 minutes in pre-set hot oven.

When the buns are cool, spread a little coffee icing on the top of each, or split down one side and fill with a little coffee butter cream.

Date bread

2 oz butter
6 oz soft brown sugar
$\frac{1}{4}$ pint water
1 egg (well beaten)
8 oz plain flour
$\frac{1}{2}$ teaspoon salt
1 teaspoon bicarbonate of soda
3 oz stoned dates

2-lb loaf tin (8 $\frac{1}{2}$ inches by 4 $\frac{1}{2}$ inches by 2 $\frac{1}{2}$ inches)

Method
Grease the loaf tin and set the oven at 350°F or Mark 4. Melt the butter and brown sugar in the $\frac{1}{4}$ pint water, allow to cool and then pour on to the beaten egg. Sieve the flour with salt and bicarbonate of soda into a mixing bowl, make a well in the centre and pour into it the liquid ingredients ; add dates and stir until smooth. Pour mixture into the tin and bake for about 50 minutes in the pre-set oven.

English cakes

There are a great variety of ways to make English cakes, but whichever recipe you choose, one of the most important aspects is the initial preparation. The success and impact of a home-baked cake in flavour, texture and appearance hinge on this factor.

Flavour and texture are dependent on the choice and preparation of the right ingredients. Don't gaily substitute plain for self-raising flour and then complain when you get a sad cake, and do mix ingredients thoroughly in the early stages.

Appearance depends largely on neat and expert preparation of the cake tin. Cut lining paper to fit exactly ; if it has lumps and bumps the finished cake will be bumpy to match.

Preparation of ingredients

Flour should always be sifted with a good pinch of salt before use. Sifting aerates the flour and removes any small lumps ; the salt improves the flavour.

Keep both plain and self-raising flour in your cupboard so that you can use whichever is indicated in a recipe.

Fats play a large part in the success of each cake, and different kinds are suitable for different recipes. Butter is the perfect fat for cake-making because it gives a wonderful flavour and improves the keeping properties of the cake. Margarine, which is easier to cream, can be used in place of butter in nearly every recipe.

Shortening, or a cooking compound, gives very good results, particularly where the proportion of sugar and liquid in the recipe is high. These lard or vegetable fats contain no curd, and if stored properly will keep for many months.

A good beef dripping gives excellent results for plain luncheon cakes, but before use it must be clarified in the following way : turn the dripping into a bowl and pour on an equal amount of boiling water. Stir well, then leave it to set. Remove the solidified fat, scrape away any impurities from the underneath and then heat

71

it gently until it no longer bubbles. Pour into an enamel basin and leave to set.

Sugars are very important. Using the wrong type will completely spoil a cake. Fine caster sugar must be used for all creamed cake mixtures. A coarse sugar results in cakes with spotted tops. Granulated sugar can be used for all mixtures which are 'rubbed in'. Demerara sugar should only be used in recipes where the sugar is dissolved and added to the cake mixture in liquid form, eg. gingerbread made by using the 'warming' method.

Soft brown sugar is good for luncheon and fruit cakes, Barbados sugar (dark brown, rich and moist) is used for rich fruit, wedding, birthday and Christmas cakes to improve the flavour. Some recipes may replace Barbados sugar with caster sugar and black treacle mixed together.

Eggs are essential to make cakes light. They expand and coagulate on heating and so trap any air which is beaten into the mixture.

Fruit, nuts and candied peel All dried fruit, unless clearly marked as washed and ready for use, should be cleaned. Gritty fruit can spoil the texture and the flavour of the cake.

When using nuts, check the recipe to see whether they should be shredded, flaked or chopped. This seemingly small variation has a decided effect on flavour, texture and appearance, particularly when the nuts are used to finish the cake.

Choose candied peel in caps : as a rule it is softer and fuller in flavour than the chopped variety. Scoop out the sugar from the centre and then shred the peel on a grater. This way you obtain the very best flavour and the fine slivers look attractive in the finished cake.

Raising agents Baking powder is a commercial preparation made up of two parts cream of tartar and one part bicarbonate of soda. It should be sifted with plain flour in the proportion given in the recipe.

Bicarbonate of soda can be used instead, combined with soured milk, buttermilk, vinegar or black treacle. The proportions to replace 2 teaspoons of baking powder are $\frac{1}{2}$ teaspoon bicarbonate of soda to $\frac{1}{3}$ pint soured milk or buttermilk. This is only suitable for scones or very plain cake mixtures as the proportion of liquid is so high. Use $\frac{1}{2}$ teaspoon bicarbonate of soda plus 1 tablespoon vinegar or black treacle for everyday fruit cakes.

Sifting 8 oz plain flour with 2 level teaspoons of baking powder gives the same result as using self-raising flour.

Ways of mixing

Rubbing-in method This is used for small cakes and luncheon cakes. These are always meant to be eaten fresh, or at least within 2-3 days of baking. The fat is cut in small pieces, added to sifted flour, then rubbed lightly with the fingertips until it resembles fine breadcrumbs.

Warming (or boiled) method This is suited to gingerbread, Yorkshire parkin and some fruit cakes. A variety of raising agents is used with this method and as a general rule the texture is damp and close and so will improve with keeping.

Fat, sugar and liquids are melted in a saucepan before being added to flour. The mixture before baking (called cake batter) is much thinner than ordinary mixtures and is easily poured into prepared tin.

Creaming method This is suited to all rich cakes and gives a light, even-textured cake with a soft, slightly moist top which should be smooth and perfectly flat.

For the very best results, follow these rules. First have the butter or margarine and eggs at room temperature (about 70°F). At this temperature the mixture is easier to beat and is less likely to curdle.

Beat the sugar a little at a time into the well-creamed butter, scraping the sides of the bowl once or twice during this process. If you leave any sugar crystals on the sides of the bowl, this will give the finished cake a speckled top.

When the butter and sugar look like whipped cream the eggs may be added. If the amount of sugar is **under** 8 oz the eggs should be whisked together and added a little at a time. If using **more than** 8 oz sugar, the eggs may be added one at a time. After each addition of egg the mixture must be well beaten.

Watchpoint It is at this stage that curdling is most likely to happen. It is caused either because the butter and sugar have not been thoroughly creamed, or because the eggs are very cold. This curdling can be corrected by standing the mixing bowl in a little hot water and beating vigorously. If, however, you still have more egg to add, stir in 1 tablespoon of the sifted flour with each further addition of egg.

Then, using a metal spoon, gently fold in the flour and any liquid given in the recipe. Do not beat or stir ; this will remove air beaten in and make the cake rise and crack.

Preparation of tins

Brush sides and base of shallow tins with melted fat, line base with circle of buttered grease-proof paper and dust with flour. With tins over 2 inches in depth, sides should also be lined with buttered greaseproof paper.

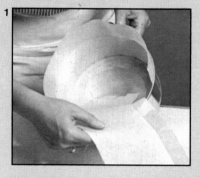

1 *Cut a strip about 1 inch longer than the circumference of tin and 1 inch wider than the depth. Fold down ½ inch on the long edge and cut slits in the fold (about ½ inch deep and 1 inch apart). This folded end of the side strip will then overlap at the base*

2 *The circular base lining will then hold this overlap in place*

Baking

First prepare the cake tins (see page 73), then turn on the oven, set the temperature and arrange the shelves before mixing the cake. There must be room for the heat to circulate in the oven round baking sheets and cake tins, otherwise the underneath of the cakes will burn.

If you are baking more than one cake in an oven that has back burners or elements, arrange the cakes side by side. If you have an oven with side burners, arrange the cakes back and front. A centre shelf is the best position for baking a cake.

Do not move the cake until the mixture is set and avoid opening the oven door until the minimum time given in the recipe is reached. This is a guide to cooking time but you should always test a cake before removing it from the oven. Creamed cake mixtures should spring back when pressed lightly with the fingertips. Fruit cakes are tested by piercing with a trussing needle or fine skewer which should come away clean.

Victoria sandwich

about 6 oz butter
about 6 oz caster sugar
3 large eggs
about 6 oz self-raising flour
pinch of salt
1-2 tablespoons milk

To finish
**3 tablespoons warm jam, or lemon
    curd**
caster sugar (for dredging)

Deep 8-inch diameter sandwich tin

To make a good Victoria sandwich, weigh eggs in their
shells and use exact equivalent
of butter, sugar and flour.

Method
Grease and line sandwich tin ;
set the oven at 350°F or Mark 4.

Using the creaming method,
soften the butter in a bowl, add
the sugar and cream them together until soft and light.
Whisk the eggs, add a little at a
time and then beat thoroughly.
Sift the flour with the salt and
fold into the mixture a third at

a time, adding enough milk to
make the mixture drop easily
from the spoon. Spread the
mixture in the prepared tin and
bake in pre-set oven for about
40-45 minutes.

To test if cake is ready press
lightly with fingertips and it
should spring back. The colour
should be golden-brown, and
the cake shrink from sides of
the tin. Have two wire cooling
racks ready, and put a folded
clean tea towel or double
thickness of absorbent paper
on one of them. Loosen the
sides of the cake with a
round-bladed knife, place the
rack with the towel or paper on
top of the cake (towel next to
it) and turn over ; remove the
tin and disc of paper from the
base. Place second rack on top
of cake base and carefully and
quickly turn it over again. This
prevents the cake having the
marks of cake rack on its top.

When the cake is cool split
in half, fill with jam or lemon
curd ; dust top with caster sugar.

Rich almond cake

4 oz butter
5 oz caster sugar
3 eggs
3 oz ground almonds
1½ oz plain flour
2-3 drops of almond essence

Deep 7-inch diameter sandwich tin

Method

Grease and flour sandwich tin, cover base with disc of grease-proof paper ; set the oven at 350°F or Mark 4.

Soften butter with a wooden spoon in a bowl, add the sugar a tablespoon at a time, and beat thoroughly until mixture is soft and light. Add the eggs, one at a time, adding one-third of the almonds with each egg. Beat well. Fold in the flour and almond essence with a metal spoon and turn cake mixture into the prepared tin.

Bake in pre-set oven for 45-50 minutes until cake is cooked. (Test by inserting a thin skewer ; it should come out clean.) When cooked, the cake should also shrink very slightly from the sides of the tin.

To turn out, have ready two wire cooling racks, put a clean folded tea towel or single thickness of absorbent paper on one of them. Loosen the sides of the cake with a round-bladed knife, place the rack with the towel or paper on top of the cake (towel next to it) and turn over ; remove the tin and disc of paper from the base.

Place second rack on top of cake base and carefully and quickly turn it over again. This prevents rack marking top of cake. Dust with caster sugar.

Rich almond cake is good on its own or with a fruit compote

English madeleines

Victoria sandwich mixture with about
  2 eggs and equivalent weights of
  butter, caster sugar and self-
  raising flour (about 4 oz of each)
  — see method, page 75
2-3 drops of vanilla essence
4 tablespoons apricot, or redcurrant, glaze (see page 152)
6 tablespoons desiccated coconut
8 glacé cherries

14-16 dariole moulds, or castle tins

Method
Grease moulds or tins well, and
dust with flour. Set the oven at
375°F or Mark 5.

Prepare sponge mixture,
flavour with vanilla essence
and half fill the moulds or
tins. Bake for 8-10 minutes
until golden-brown.

When the cakes are cool, trim
the tops to give them a flat
surface when inverted. Turn
them upside down and spear
each separately on a fork. Then
brush with warm glaze, roll at
once in the desiccated coconut,
decorate with half a glacé cherry.

Cherry and walnut cake

6 oz butter
6 oz caster sugar
3 eggs
8 oz self-raising flour
pinch of salt
4 oz glacé cherries (halved)
2 oz walnuts (shelled and chopped)
1-2 tablespoons milk

7-inch diameter cake tin

Method
Prepare cake tin and set the
oven at 350°F or Mark 4.

Cream the butter until soft
in a bowl, add the sugar and
continue beating until the
mixture is light. Whisk the eggs
and beat them in a little at a
time. Sift the flour with the salt
and mix 2 tablespoons with the
prepared cherries and walnuts.
Fold in the flour one-third at a
time, adding the cherries, walnuts and milk at the end.

Turn into the prepared tin and
bake in the pre-set oven for
1-1$\frac{1}{4}$ hours. Cake is ready when
a trussing needle or fine skewer
comes away clean.

Rice cake

4 oz butter
grated rind of ½ lemon
8 oz caster sugar
4 eggs
8 oz ground rice

7-inch diameter cake tin

Method

Prepare cake tin and set the oven at 350°F or Mark 4.

Cream the butter until soft with the lemon rind in a bowl, add the sugar and continue beating until light ; separate the eggs and beat in the yolks one at a time.

Whisk the egg whites until stiff and then fold into the mixture with the ground rice. Turn into the prepared tin and bake in the pre-set oven for about 1 hour. To test if cake is ready, press lightly with the fingertips — it should spring back.

Seed cake

4 oz butter
4 oz caster sugar
3 eggs (well beaten)
6½ oz self-raising flour
pinch of salt
2-3 tablespoons milk
2 teaspoons caraway seeds

6-inch diameter cake tin

Method

Prepare cake tin and set the oven at 350°F or Mark 4.

Cream the butter until soft, add the sugar and beat together until light and fluffy. Add the beaten eggs a little at a time. Sift the flour with the salt, fold one-third of the flour into the fat mixture and then add the remainder with the milk and caraway seeds.

Turn the mixture into the prepared tin and bake in the pre-set oven for about 1-1¼ hours. To test if cake is ready, press lightly with the fingertips — it should spring back.

Rock cakes

8 oz self-raising flour
pinch of salt
4 oz butter
3 oz caster sugar
3-4 oz sultanas
1 oz candied peel (finely chopped, or shredded)
2 eggs
1-2 tablespoons milk

Method

Grease a baking tin and set the oven at 425°F or Mark 7.

Sift the flour with the salt into a bowl, add the butter, cut it into the flour with a round-bladed knife. Then, using your finger tips, rub it in until the mixture resembles fine breadcrumbs. Stir in the sugar, sultanas and peel.

Whisk the eggs to a froth and add them to the dry ingredients with a fork, adding as much milk as necessary to bind the dry ingredients together. Put out in tablespoons on to the prepared tin and bake at once in pre-set oven for about 15 minutes.

Watchpoint The mixture should hold its shape — if too much milk is added the cakes lose their rock-like appearance.

Cider and nut cake

4 oz butter
4 oz caster sugar
2 eggs (well beaten)
$1\frac{1}{2}$ oz walnuts (chopped)
8 oz plain flour
1 teaspoon bicarbonate of soda
$\frac{1}{4}$ nutmeg (grated)
1 teacup cider

For filling
2 oz butter
3 oz dates (stoned and chopped)
2 tablespoons honey
squeeze of lemon juice

Shallow 7-inch diameter cake tin

Method

Set oven at 375°F or Mark 5.

To prepare cake : beat butter and sugar to a thick cream ; add eggs and walnuts, then add half of the flour, sifted with the soda and nutmeg. Beat cider to a really good froth, pour it over this mixture and mix thoroughly. Stir in the remainder of the flour, turn into well-greased tin and bake in pre-set hot oven for 45 minutes.

Meanwhile make the filling : cream butter well and add dates, honey and lemon juice.

When cake has cooled, split in 3 and sandwich with filling.

Madeira cake

200g

8 oz butter
grated rind of $\frac{1}{2}$ lemon
10 oz caster sugar
5 eggs
13 oz plain flour
pinch of salt
1 rounded teaspoon baking powder
1 teacup milk
slice of candied citron peel

8-inch diameter cake tin

Method
Prepare the cake tin and set the oven at 350°F or Mark 4.

Cream the butter with the grated lemon rind in a bowl, add the sugar gradually and continue beating until the mixture is light and soft. Beat in the eggs one at a time, each with 1 dessertspoon of flour, and then sift the remaining flour with the salt and baking powder and fold into the mixture with the milk. Turn into the prepared tin and bake in pre-set oven for about $1\frac{1}{2}$ hours.

After the first 30 minutes place the slice of citron peel on top of the cake, and after 1 hour reduce the heat to 325°F or Mark 3. To test if cake is done, press lightly with fingertips — it should spring back.

Coconut buns

8 oz self-raising flour
pinch of salt
3 oz butter
3 oz caster sugar
3 tablespoons desiccated coconut
1 egg
2-3 tablespoons milk
$\frac{1}{2}$ teaspoon vanilla essence

9-bun tin

Method
Grease tin and set the oven at 400°F or Mark 6.

Sift the flour with the salt into a bowl and rub in the fat very finely. Add the sugar and coconut and mix well together. Beat the egg with the milk and vanilla essence, add to the dry ingredients and mix with a wooden spoon until smooth.

Spoon mixture into the prepared tin, a tablespoon for each bun, and bake in the pre-set oven for 20-25 minutes, until a fine skewer pressed into a bun comes away clean.

Raisin dripping cake

1 lb plain flour
$\frac{1}{2}$ teaspoon salt
6 oz dripping
8 oz raisins
2 oz candied peel
6 oz granulated sugar
1 tablespoon black treacle
about $\frac{1}{2}$ pint milk
2 eggs (beaten)
1 teaspoon bicarbonate of soda

8-inch square cake tin

Method

Prepare cake tin and set oven at 350°F or Mark 4.

Sift the flour with the salt into a bowl and rub in the dripping thoroughly.

Remove stones from raisins, shred the candied peel and add these to the flour with the sugar.

Warm the treacle in a quarter of the milk, mix this with the beaten eggs and stir into the cake mixture with enough cold milk to make a dough of dropping consistency, ie. that will just drop from the wooden spoon when shaken.

Next add the bicarbonate of soda (dissolved in 1 tablespoon milk), put mixture into the prepared tin immediately and bake in pre-set oven for $1\frac{1}{2}$-2 hours, reducing the temperature to 325°F or Mark 3 after the first hour. Cake is ready when a fine skewer pressed into cake comes away clean.

This cake is good thinly sliced or cut into squares and buttered.

Sultana and cherry cake

$1\frac{1}{2}$ lb sultanas
12 oz glacé cherries
8 oz plain flour
pinch of salt
6 oz butter
grated rind of $\frac{1}{2}$ lemon
6 oz caster sugar
4 eggs

8-inch diameter cake tin

Method

Prepare cake tin, set oven at 350°F or Mark 4.

Clean sultanas ; if cherries are very sticky put in a strainer and wash quickly with hot water. When dry, cut cherries in half, mix with sultanas and one-third of the flour, sifted with a pinch of salt.

Soften butter with lemon rind, add sugar and beat until soft and light. Whisk eggs, add a little at a time, then stir in half of remaining flour. Fold in fruit, then last portion of flour. Turn into prepared tin and bake in pre-set oven for 1 hour, then reduce heat to 325°F or Mark 3 ; continue cooking about 1 hour and test by inserting a fine skewer, which should come away clean.

Walnut bread

4 oz granulated sugar
6 oz golden syrup
small teacup milk (scant ⅓ pint)
2 oz sultanas
8 oz plain flour
pinch of salt
3 teaspoons baking powder
2 oz walnuts (roughly chopped)
1 egg (beaten)

*Loaf tin, 8½ inches by 4¼ inches by
2½ inches deep*

Method
Grease and flour loaf tin, set oven at 350°F or Mark 4.

Heat the sugar, syrup, milk and sultanas in a saucepan and stir gently until the sugar is dissolved ; allow to cool.

Sift the flour, salt and baking powder into bowl and add the roughly chopped walnuts. Tip the sugar and syrup mixture on to the beaten egg and then pour into the middle of the dry ingredients and stir until smooth. Pour into the prepared tin and bake in pre-set oven for about 1½ hours. Press cake lightly with fingertips ; if it springs back, it is done.

Cheese tartlets
(Welsh cheese cakes)

4 oz quantity rich shortcrust pastry
    (see page 154)

For filling
Victoria sandwich mixture with about
    1 egg and equivalent weights of
    butter, caster sugar and self-
    raising flour (about 2 oz each) —
    see method, page 75
1-2 tablespoons jam
1-2 drops of vanilla essence
caster sugar (for dredging)

12 tartlet tins

Method
Prepare the pastry, roll thinly and line tartlet tins. Set oven at 400°F or Mark 6.

Put a little jam in each tartlet and prepare the sponge mixture, flavouring it with vanilla essence. Fill each pastry case with 1 teaspoon of the mixture, put in pre-set oven and bake for about 20 minutes until golden-brown.

Dust with caster sugar and eat hot or cold.

Gingerbread

4 oz butter
8 oz golden syrup
3 oz granulated sugar
1 tablespoon orange marmalade
$\frac{1}{4}$ pint milk
4 oz self-raising flour
pinch of salt
1 teaspoon ground ginger
1 teaspoon mixed spice
$\frac{1}{2}$ teaspoon bicarbonate of soda
4 oz wholemeal flour
2 small eggs (well beaten)

8-inch square cake tin

Method
Prepare tin and set the oven at 325°F or Mark 3.

Heat the butter, syrup, sugar, marmalade and milk together in a saucepan and stir gently until the sugar dissolves. Allow the mixture to cool a little. Meanwhile sift the self-raising flour with the salt, spices and soda into a mixing bowl, add the wholemeal flour and then mix together.

Add the butter and syrup mixture to the beaten eggs and then pour into the dry ingredients. Stir with a wooden spoon until a smooth batter is formed, then pour into the prepared tin and bake in pre-set oven for about $1\frac{1}{2}$ hours. Gingerbread is ready when pressed with fingertips and it springs back into place.

This gingerbread has a nice spongy texture and is cut into squares for serving.

Gingerbread foundation

1 lb plain flour
1 tablespoon bicarbonate of soda
$\frac{1}{2}$ teaspoon salt
1 dessertspoon ground ginger
$\frac{1}{2}$ teaspoon ground cinnamon
4 oz butter
8 oz soft brown sugar
1 teacup black treacle
about 2 tablespoons evaporated milk

Method
Sift the flour with the soda, salt and spices into a mixing bowl.

Place the butter, sugar and treacle in a saucepan and stir over gentle heat until dissolved. Allow this to cool a little, then mix it into the flour with enough evaporated milk to give a firm dough.

Chill the mixture for 30 minutes before rolling out and shaping as required (see overleaf).

Gingerbread men

gingerbread foundation (see page 83)

For decoration
currants
glacé cherries
white royal icing (see page 97)

Forcing bag and writing tube

The 1 lb quantity of foundation makes 3-4 dozen gingerbread men, about $3\frac{1}{2}$ inches high.

Method
Set oven at 325°F or Mark 3. Grease several baking sheets.

Roll out the mixture a good $\frac{1}{4}$ inch thick. Cut out a cardboard gingerbread man pattern; grease the underside, lay it on the dough and cut round it with a small sharp knife. When all the gingerbread men are cut, lift them up carefully with a palette knife and place them on the prepared baking sheets. Press currants in to make the eyes and waistcoat buttons and a small piece of glacé cherry for the mouth.

Bake in pre-set oven for 10-15 minutes; cool slightly and then carefully remove them from the baking sheet. With a little white icing and a writing tube, outline eyebrows, nose, tie, belt, cuffs and shoes.

Gingerbread house and gingerbread men are very popular with children

84

Gingerbread house

gingerbread foundation (see page 83)
little sugar syrup (see page 155)
royal icing (see page 97)

Forcing bag and writing nozzle

Set oven at 325°F or Mark 3. Grease several baking sheets.

Cut out a paper guide as follows : for long walls, 1 rectangle 5 inches by 10 inches ; for roof, 1 rectangle 4 inches by 10 inches ; for side walls, 1 piece, basically 5 inches square rising to a gable with 4-inch sides ; for chimney, a 2-inch square.

Roll out gingerbread to about $\frac{1}{8}$ inch thick. Use paper guide to cut out 4 walls, 2 roof pieces and 4 chimney pieces. Place sections carefully on baking sheets and bake in pre-set oven for 10-15 minutes.

When cold, using the forcing bag and writing tube, decorate with royal icing, marking the windows and doors, and the tiles on the roof. Join the pieces together by dipping the edges in sugar syrup boiled to 280°F. **Note :** cut V-shaped pieces out of base of side-pieces of chimney so that it fits on roof.

Then cover the joins with icing, using forcing bag without the writing pipe.

Strawberry walnut cream cake

3 eggs
scant 4 oz caster sugar
3 oz plain flour
2 oz walnuts (coarsely chopped)
2 tablespoons coffee essence

For filling
8-10 fl oz double cream (lightly
  whipped)
1 lb strawberries

Deep 8-inch diameter cake tin

Method
Prepare the tin by greasing and dusting out with caster sugar and flour. Set the oven at 350°F or Mark 4.

To prepare the cake mixture : whisk the eggs and sugar over heat as for a whisked sponge (see sponge cake, page 121), or combine using an electric mixer. When really thick and mousse-like, take off the heat and continue to whisk for a further minute. Sift the flour and fold it in with the walnuts and coffee essence. Turn the cake mixture into the tin and bake in the pre-set oven for 40-45 minutes.

Turn cake out to cool and when cold split into three and layer with two-thirds of the lightly whipped cream mixed with the sliced strawberries. (Reserve a few strawberries for decoration.) The filling should be really lavish. Spread the rest of the cream over the top of the cake and decorate with the reserved strawberries.

Grandmother's pound cake

8 oz butter
8 oz soft brown sugar
4 eggs (separated)
3 tablespoons sherry, or brandy, or rum
8 oz plain flour
pinch of salt
$\frac{1}{2}$ teaspoon mixed spice
$\frac{1}{2}$ teaspoon grated nutmeg
8 oz currants (cleaned)
8 oz raisins (stoned and cleaned)
8 oz sultanas (cleaned)
2 oz glacé cherries (halved)
2 oz almonds (blanched and shredded)
2 oz candied peel (shredded)

To finish
$1\frac{1}{4}$ lb almond paste (see page 96)
1-$1\frac{1}{2}$ lb fondant, or royal, icing (see pages 153 and 97)

8-inch diameter cake tin

Method

Set oven at 325°F or Mark 3. Line cake tin with a double thickness of greaseproof paper.

Soften the butter in a bowl with a wooden spoon, add the sugar and beat thoroughly until soft and light. Then beat egg yolks into the butter with the sherry (or spirit).

Sift the flour with salt and spices and divide it into three portions. Very lightly fold one into butter and egg mixture and mix second portion with the prepared fruit, glacé cherries, almonds and candied peel. Whisk egg whites until stiff; add fruit to butter mixture, then fold in the remaining portion of flour and the egg whites. Turn mixture into the prepared tin and bake in pre-set oven for about $2\frac{1}{2}$ hours.

Test if the cake is cooked by piercing with a trussing needle (or fine skewer), which should come away clean. Turn cake out of tin to cool.

To decorate the cake, cover with almond paste, and royal icing as described on pages 96-97 and pipe on decorations. Alternatively, if you decide not to pipe on decoration, simply smooth the royal icing over the marzipan, then 'rough' the top with the flat of a palette knife.

Battenburg cake

3 **egg Victoria sandwich mixture
  (see page 75)**
few drops of carmine colouring
2 **tablespoons apricot glaze (see
  page 152)**
1½ **lb almond paste (see page 96)**

*2 tins, or paper cases, each 10 inches
by 3 inches by 1½ inches deep*

Method
Place greaseproof paper in bottom of tins. Grease tins, or paper cases, and dust with flour. Set the oven at 350°F or Mark 4.

Prepare the Victoria sandwich mixture and, before filling into tins, divide it in two and colour one portion pale pink with carmine. Bake each colour in a separate tin in the pre-set moderate oven for 15-20 minutes. When cool, trim each cake and cut in two lengthways. Brush the strips of cake with some of the warm apricot glaze and join them together again with one pink strip above a natural colour one (and vice-versa) to make a square of alternate colours.

Roll the almond paste into an oblong the length of the re-shaped cake and wide enough to wrap right round it, leaving the square ends exposed. First brush the top of the cake with apricot glaze and place cake, inverted, on the almond paste; then brush the remaining three sides with glaze and press the almond paste round, arranging the join neatly down one side.

Using your fingers or pastry pincers, crimp the edges of the cake and decorate the top with criss-cross scoring.

Joining the four strips of Victoria sandwich cake together with apricot glaze to give the chequered effect, characteristic of a Battenburg

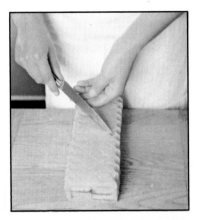

Brushing the long sides of the re-shaped cake with warm apricot glaze before wrapping the almond paste round, leaving the ends open

After crimping the edges of the Battenburg cake with fingers or pincers, decorate top with criss-cross scoring using back of a knife

Lemon whisky cake

3 eggs
weight of above eggs in butter, caster sugar, self-raising flour (well sifted)
6 oz sultanas (washed)
pared rind of 1 large lemon
2½ fl oz whisky

7-inch diameter cake tin

Method
Infuse the lemon rind in the whisky in a covered glass for 24 hours before use.

Prepare the cake tin by greasing and flouring. Set the oven at 350°F or Mark 4.

Cream the butter, add sugar gradually and beat until light and fluffy. Separate the eggs and add the yolks to the butter and sugar, one at a time, beating well. Stir in the sultanas, the strained whisky and half the flour.

Whip the egg whites to a firm snow and fold into the mixture with the remainder of the flour. Turn mixture into the tin and bake in the pre-set moderate oven for 50-60 minutes.

Luncheon plum cake

12 oz butter
12 oz caster sugar
5 eggs
1 lb plain flour
½ teaspoon salt
½ teaspoon mixed spice
¼ teaspoon grated nutmeg
8 oz sultanas (stoned and cleaned)
8 oz currants (cleaned)
6 oz raisins (cleaned)
1 teaspoon bicarbonate of soda
½ teacup orange and lemon squash (mixed)
milk (see method)

To finish (optional)
1½ lb almond paste (see page 96)
2 lb fondant, or royal, icing (see pages 153 and 97)

9-10 inch diameter cake tin

Method
Set oven at 325°F or Mark 3. Line cake tin with double thickness of greaseproof paper.

Soften the butter, add the sugar and beat until light and fluffy. Then beat in the eggs one at a time.

Sift the flour with the salt and spices and divide it into three portions : mix one portion with the prepared fruit, sift the second with the bicarbonate of soda and stir the third into the butter mixture. Fold in the fruit and flour with the squash, then add remaining flour with enough milk to give a dropping consistency. Turn cake mixture into the prepared tin and bake in pre-set oven for 2-2½ hours.

Cakes for special occasions

Most cooks build up their personal repertoire of cake recipes which they know can be relied on to turn out well. But there is always a time — Christmas, birthdays, anniversaries and so on — when an extra-special recipe is called for. This chapter provides for just those occasions.

In the British tradition, many of these special cakes are rich fruit cakes and each has its own appropriate decoration. Don't forget, though, that all fruit cakes improve with keeping ; and the richer the cake, the longer it should be kept. So these are definitely recipes for

planned celebrations, not last-minute parties. Each of the fruit cake recipes suggests how long the cake should be kept before eating, but you should never ice a cake more than a week before eating. Otherwise the icing tends to harden and discolour.

Quite a large part of this chapter is devoted to decorating your cakes — the techniques of piping and shaping icing and marzipan. Once you have mastered the shapes suggested here you will have acquired a certain amount of expertise with your materials and can go on to experiment with your own designs.

Golden wedding cake

1 lb golden sultanas, or white
   raisins (cleaned)
8 oz citron peel (shredded)
4 oz glacé cherries (halved)
4 oz candied pineapple (chopped)
4 oz candied lemon peel (chopped)
4 oz almonds (chopped)
4 oz walnuts (chopped)
8 oz butter
10 oz caster sugar
4 eggs
4 tablespoons orange jelly
   marmalade
12 oz self-raising flour
1 teaspoon salt
1 teaspoon ground cinnamon
$\frac{1}{2}$ teacup milk
$\frac{1}{2}$ teaspoon vanilla essence

For decoration
apricot glaze (see page 152)
2 lb almond paste (see page 100)
3 lb royal icing (coloured pale, and
   golden, yellow) — see page 101

*8-9 inch diameter cake tin : forcing
bag, No. 2 plain pipe and shell
pipe*

This cake should be made 2-3
weeks before it is iced.

Method
Grease tin and line it with
greaseproof paper. Grease and
flour paper. Set the oven at
300°F or Mark 2.
  Mix the prepared fruit, peel
and nuts together. Cream the
butter thoroughly in a mixing
bowl ; add the sugar and beat
again until soft and light. Beat
in the eggs, one at a time,
and then stir in the marmalade.
Sift the flour with salt and
cinnamon and fold into the
mixture with the milk, vanilla
essence and the mixed fruit and
nuts. Turn the mixture into the
tin and bake in the pre-set oven

for about $2\frac{1}{2}$-3 hours.
  When the cake is cold, wrap
and store for about 2-3 weeks
to mellow. Then brush with
apricot glaze, cover with almond paste and leave for 1-2
days. Coat with pale yellow royal
icing, pipe on the date of the
wedding in golden yellow and
decorate with a golden rose
and butterfly. Finish with a
shell edging and a golden ribbon.
Note. Instructions for covering
cake with almond paste and
royal icing are given on pages
96-97.

*Pale yellow icing with darker gold
decorations for a golden wedding*

Christmas cake

8 oz plain flour
pinch of salt
½ teaspoon ground cinnamon
½ nutmeg (grated)
1 lb sultanas
12 oz seeded raisins
8 oz glacé cherries
4 oz almonds (blanched and
  shredded) — see page 154
2 oz candied peel (shredded)
6 oz butter
grated rind of ½ lemon, or orange
6 oz dark brown sugar (Barbados)
4 eggs (beaten)
2 tablespoons brandy, or rum, or
  sherry, or 1 tablespoon orange
  juice

8-inch diameter cake tin

This cake should be made 2-3 weeks before it is iced.

Method
Line the cake tin with double thickness of greaseproof paper ; set oven at 350°F or Mark 4.

Sift the flour with the salt and spices into bowl, then divide mixture into three portions. Mix one portion with the prepared fruit, almonds and peel.

Beat the butter until soft, add the lemon or orange rind and sugar and continue beating until the mixture is very soft. Add the eggs one at a time, beating well between each one, then use a metal spoon to fold in a second portion of flour. Mix in the fruit and then the remaining flour, spirit, sherry or fruit juice.

Turn the mixture into the prepared tin and smooth the top of the cake. Dip your fingers in warm water and moisten the surface very slightly.

Watchpoint This can be done with a pastry brush but great care must be taken as there should be only a film of water on the mixture. In baking, the small quantity of steam from the water prevents the crust of the cake getting hard during the long cooking.

Put the cake in the middle of the pre-set oven and bake for about 2¼ hours. After 1 hour reduce the heat of the oven to 325°F or Mark 3 and cover the top with a double thickness of greaseproof paper.

Test the cake after 2 hours' cooking by sticking a trussing needle or fine skewer in the centre. If it comes out quite clean the cake is done. Allow the cake to cool for about 30 minutes in the tin and then turn it on to a rack and leave until quite cold.

Wrap the cake in greaseproof paper or foil and store it in an airtight container before decorating. It improves with keeping, but should not be iced more than a week before Christmas. Use glacé icing to ice cake and royal icing to decorate (see following pages).

Almond paste

8 oz ground almonds
6 oz caster sugar
4 oz icing sugar (finely sifted)
1 egg
1 tablespoon lemon juice
1 tablespoon brandy, or sherry, or extra lemon juice
$\frac{1}{2}$ teaspoon vanilla essence
2 drops of almond essence
2 teaspoons orange flower water, or little extra sherry, or lemon juice
apricot glaze (see page 152)

Method
Place the almonds, caster sugar and icing sugar in a bowl and mix them together. Whisk the egg with the lemon juice and other flavourings and add this to the mixture of almonds and sugar, pounding lightly to release a little of the almond oil. Knead with your hands until the paste is smooth.

Brush or spread the cake thinly with hot apricot glaze. This coating makes sure that the almond paste will stick to the cake. Now place the almond paste on top of the cake ; roll it over the top so that it falls down the sides (see photographs below).

Dust your hands with icing sugar and smooth the paste firmly and evenly on to the sides of the cake. Turn it upside down, press to flatten the paste on the top and roll the rolling pin round the sides. This gives a clean, sharp edge to the paste. Leave the cake in a tin for 2-3 days before icing.

Note For a guide to quanties of almond paste and icing, see page 153.

Almond paste is laid on top of the previously-glazed cake, and rolled with a rolling pin so that it falls over the edges and down the sides

Having smoothed the almond paste firmly and evenly on the sides, turn cake upside down and roll round sides to give a clean, sharp edge

Royal icing

1 lb icing sugar
2 egg whites

This icing is not suitable for flat icing on sponge cakes because it would be too hard. A softer royal icing is given on page 101.

Method

Finely sift the icing sugar. Whisk the egg whites until frothy and add the icing sugar 1 tablespoon at a time, beating thoroughly between each addition. Continue this beating until the mixture will stand in peaks. Add flavouring and colour if wished. Keep the bowl covered with a damp cloth when piping.

Covering a cake with royal icing is less difficult if a cake-stand with a revolving turntable is used. Use a spatula to smooth sides

Glacé icing

4-5 tablespoons granulated sugar
$\frac{1}{4}$ pint water
8-12 oz icing sugar (finely sifted)
flavouring essence (and colouring
  as required — see page 153)

Method

Make sugar syrup by dissolving sugar in $\frac{1}{4}$ pint of water in a small saucepan. Bring to the boil, and boil steadily for 10 minutes. Remove pan from the heat and when quite cold, add the icing sugar, 1 tablespoon at a time, and beat thoroughly with a wooden spatula. The icing should coat back of spoon and look very glossy. Warm the pan gently on a very low heat. (You should be able to touch the bottom of the pan with the palm of your hand.)

Flavour and colour icing, spread over cake with a palette knife.

Allow sides of the cake to dry before roughly spreading icing over top of the cake with a plastic or metal 'straight edge' ruler (or palette knife)

97

Wedding cake

3 lb sultanas
3 lb currants
1 lb seedless raisins
1 lb muscatel raisins (seeded)
8 oz glacé cherries (halved)
4 oz almonds (blanched and
    shredded) — see page 154
8 oz candied peel (finely shredded)
10 fl oz brandy
2½ lb plain flour
1 teaspoon salt
1 teaspoon ground cinnamon
1 nutmeg (grated)
1 tablespoon cocoa
2 lb butter
grated rind of 1 lemon and 1 orange
2 lb caster sugar
1 tablespoon black treacle
18 eggs
4 oz ground almonds

Cake tins (for sizes see page 103)

This amount will make a two-tiered cake using 12-inch and 8-inch round tins. If adapting this recipe for square cake tins, remember that they hold rather more mixture than the round ones, and a tiered cake (made with square tins) looks better if the tiers are not too deep.

This is a rich cake and is best made three months before the wedding day.

Method

Prepare the cake tins, lining them with 4-5 thicknesses of greaseproof paper and tying a stout band of brown paper, or several thicknesses of newspaper, round the outside of the large tins so that the paper stands up about 2 inches round the rim. Don't grease inside paper at all as the cake mixture is very rich and will not stick.

Clean and prepare the fruit : place all in a large basin and sprinkle with half the brandy. cover and leave for 24 hours. Stir several times during this period so that the fruit soaks up all the liquid.

Sift the flour with the salt, spices and cocoa and then mix one-third of it with the prepared fruit. Cream the butter until soft, add the grated orange and lemon rind, and the sugar, and beat thoroughly until light and fluffy. It is best to beat with your hand for this quantity if an electric mixer is not available. Stir in the black treacle and beat in the eggs one at a time. Fold in the ground almonds and half the remaining flour, add the fruit and brandy mixture and lastly the rest of the flour. Turn into the prepared tins ready for baking, smooth the top with a palette knife and brush over with a little water. This helps to keep the cake soft on top in spite of the long baking.

For baking the cake the oven should be pre-set at 325°F or Mark 3. See the chart, page 103, for baking times. To keep cakes moist during baking, set large tins on several thicknesses of newspaper, and small tins inside a larger empty tin. This prevents the cakes from drying out.

Cover the cakes with a double thickness of brown paper when they are nicely coloured and reduce the heat to 300°F or Mark 2 after 3 hours.

It is quite possible to bake a two-tiered cake in a domestic oven, placing the smaller tin on a shelf above the large bottom tier, but if three cakes are being made it is better to bake the bottom tier first and ▶

then the two smaller cakes. The uncooked mixture will not spoil if left in the tins overnight in a cool larder or refrigerator.

After baking, leave the cakes to cool in their tins for 30 minutes, and then carefully turn them on to wire racks, but leave the greaseproof paper on. When quite cold, wrap them in several more thicknesses of greaseproof paper and store in an airtight tin. The cakes are best if they are made three months before the wedding day.

During this time, say about every 4-5 weeks, unwrap the cakes, pierce them with a fine knitting needle and baste with about 5 tablespoons brandy. Rewrap and store as before. It is only necessary to pierce the cakes at the first soaking.

It is a good idea to bake an extra slab of cake for large weddings, when it is difficult to avoid a time lag between the bride cutting the cake and the guests eating it. Make this slab quite large and cover only the top with almond paste and icing. It can then be easily cut up behind the scenes, and added to the trays of cake being handed to the guests.

Almond paste

For about 2 lb quantity of marzipan
1 lb ground almonds
10 oz caster sugar
6 oz icing sugar (sifted)
1 large egg (or 2 small ones)
1 egg yolk
juice of $\frac{1}{2}$ lemon
1 tablespoon brandy, or rum, or
   sherry
$\frac{1}{2}$ teaspoon vanilla essence
2 tablespoons orange flower water
apricot glaze (see page 152)

This is a richer almond paste than the one given on page 96. The quantity required will vary a little for each cake, depending on the depth of the cake in relation to the diameter, but for a good wedding cake you will need about half the weight of the cake in marzipan. (For a guide to amounts, see chart on page 103).

Method
Place dry ingredients in a bowl and mix together ; whisk the eggs and extra yolk with remaining ingredients, add this to the mixture of almonds and sugar, pounding lightly to release a little of the almond oil. Knead this mixture with the hand until smooth.

The almond paste should be put on about one week before the icing and decoration. This gives time for the paste to set and consequently the oil from the ground almonds is less likely to seep through the icing. A wedding cake should always have at least two coats of royal icing before it is decorated, to be sure of a good white colour.

Cover 6-8$\frac{1}{2}$ inch diameter cake with the paste in the way described and illustrated on page 96.

For a larger cake it is wiser to use the following method : brush only the top of the cake with the hot apricot glaze. Roll out about half the marzipan to around the size of the cake top, using caster sugar to prevent it sticking to the slab or pastry board. Lift the cake, place it upside down on the paste and then, keeping your left hand firmly on the cake and rotating it gently, cut and mould the marzipan flush to the edge. Lift the cake over and brush away any crumbs. Take the remaining marzipan, knead it into a smooth long roll and press with the rolling pin to the depth of the cake.

Trim the edges and brush the paste with the hot glaze. Roll this strip round the cake (glazed side next to the cake) making a neat join and finish it by rolling it firmly with a straight-sided bottle or jam jar.

Royal icing

1 lb icing sugar
2 egg whites
1 teaspoon lemon juice, or orange flower water
$\frac{1}{2}$ teaspoon glycerine

Method

Pass the icing sugar through a fine nylon or hair sieve ; whisk egg whites to a froth, add icing sugar, a tablespoonful at a time, beating thoroughly between each addition. Stir in flavouring and glycerine, continue beating until icing will stand in peaks.

Keep bowl covered with a damp cloth when using icing.

This icing sets very hard and is, therefore, particularly suitable for a tiered cake or for one that is to be stored for any length of time. Give the cake at least two flat coatings of royal icing before starting the decoration. The first coat need only be quite thin and should be left in a warm airy room to dry. The next day coat again with icing and allow it to dry in the same way before decorating, as it is difficult to pipe on to a wet surface.

A very approximate guide to the quantity of icing needed is given in the chart (see page 103) The amount of icing needed, however, depends on the number and thickness of coatings and amount of decoration.

Cake boards

Choose the 'drum' type of board, ie. one that is $\frac{1}{2}$ inch thick ; for bottom tier it should be 2 inches larger than cake, measured after coating twice.

For the smaller cakes the ▶ 101

Wedding cake continued

board should be only 1 inch larger so that the decorative edging is piped close to the rim of the board. However, if the cake is to be mounted without pillars, place the second and third tiers on thin boards exactly the same size as the cakes.

Pillars, cake boards and other cake decorating equipment can be obtained by mail order from The Baker Smith School of Cake Decorating, 65 The Street, Tongham, Farnham, Surrey.

Finishing
Store each tier in a separate box away from dust. On the wedding day mount them on a silver stand, place a small spray of flowers on the top to match the bride's bouquet.

Albumen-based powder can replace egg whites, lemon juice or glycerine in royal icing. Packed in 1, 2 or 4 oz quantities, it is obtainable from Hartley Smith. To use powder : whisk with a fork in water with chill taken off until dissolved ; beat in icing sugar. 1 oz albumen powder is dissolved in $\frac{1}{2}$ pint water, which takes about $3\frac{1}{2}$ lb icing sugar.

Piping flowers

Colour one cup of royal icing bright pink. Fit a No. 58 petal pipe to a forcing bag. Spread a little of the bright pink icing down side of bag to thin end of pipe opening ; lay knife blade over this, fill up with icing and remove knife. Turn bag over so that thick end of pipe is pointing downwards.

1 *Attach 1-inch square of waxed paper to the flower spinner with icing. Turn it to form the flower centre*

2 *Pipe two more petals on to the centre piece still with the thick end of the pipe down. This will form a bud*

3 *Add a further three petals to the bud to make a medium-size flower. Make plenty of buds and flowers*

4 *For larger flowers : pipe five petals on to medium ones. Leave flowers 24 hours to dry, then remove paper*

Wedding cake quantity chart

	For 1-tier cake : Round 11-inch tin	For 1-tier cake : Square 12-inch tin	For 2-tier cake : Round or square 12-inch tin 8-inch tin	For 3-tier cake : Round or square 12-inch tin $8\frac{1}{2}$-inch tin 6-inch tin
Rich fruit cake ingredients	$\frac{1}{2}$ quantity given	$\frac{3}{4}$ quantity given	quantity given	$1\frac{1}{4}$ quantity given
Baking time	$4\frac{1}{2}$ hours	5 hours	For 12-inch cake : 5 hours For 8-inch cake : 3 hours	For 12-inch cake : 5 hours For $8\frac{1}{2}$-inch cake : $3\frac{1}{2}$ hours For 6-inch cake : $2\frac{1}{2}$ hours
For almond paste	5 lb marzipan	5–6 lb marzipan	For 12 inch cake : 5–6 lb marzipan For 8-inch cake : 2 lb marzipan	For 12-inch cake : 5–6 lb marzipan For $8\frac{1}{2}$-inch cake : 2 lb marzipan For 6-inch cake : 1 lb marzipan
For royal icing	4–6 lb icing sugar	4–6 lb icing sugar	For 12-inch cake : 4–6 lb icing sugar For 8-inch cake : $2\frac{1}{2}$–4 lb icing sugar	For 12-inch cake : 4–6 lb icing sugar For $8\frac{1}{2}$-inch cake : $2\frac{1}{2}$–4 lb icing sugar For 6-inch cake : $1\frac{1}{2}$–2 lb icing sugar

Wedding cake continued

Icing and decorating

Equipment used for cake decoration : straight-edge metal ruler, plastic scraper, turntable, flower spinner, No. 2 writing pipe, No. 58 petal pipe and No. 2 shell pipe or No. 42 scroll pipe, forcing bag.

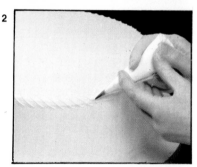

When decorating a wedding cake, use about two-thirds of the icing for coating the cake, one third for the decoration. Cover the cake with almond paste well in advance, to give the paste time to set (see page 100). Always keep the bowl covered with a damp cloth when using icing.

To coat the cake, place icing on top of cake with palette knife. Work well on cake to remove air bubbles. Holding a straight-edge metal ruler at an angle of 45°, draw it back and forth across the cake until the surface is perfect. This may take some time.

Then place the cake on a turntable. Spread the surplus icing down sides, adding more as required. Use a plastic spatula at an angle of 45° and pull cake round until icing is smooth (1) Cover the edge of the cake board in the same way.

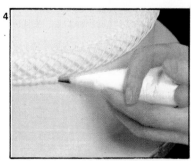

When coating is completed colour one cup of remaining icing bright pink and page flowers as illustrated on page 102. Leave to dry.

To decorate, place a No. 2 writing pipe in the forcing bag. Fill it with white icing and pipe diagonal lines round the top edge of cake at $\frac{1}{4}$-inch intervals (2) then repeat the lines in the opposite direction to form a lattice. Make the third and fourth lines of the lattice over

the original ones, but make them slightly longer than the original ones for a neat finish (3). Allow each layer of icing to dry before applying the next.

(4) Using a No. 2 shell pipe, or No. 42 scroll pipe make small shell shapes round the inner and outer edges of the lattice to cover up all the ends. Repeat the whole lattice process round the base of the cake and on the smaller tier.

With a No. 2 writing pipe, mark the rim of a 3-inch diameter cup or tumbler with small icing drops. Then press drops lightly on to top of lower tier at equal intervals to outline five circles (5). Using the same pipe, still with white icing, pipe on to side of the lower tier two loops between each circle (6), making ten loops altogether. Pipe four similar loops on side of upper tier.

Attach the flowers to the cake (7), using icing from the No. 2 writing pipe. Taking the dots on top of the cake and the loops on the side as guiding lines, arrange the flowers as shown in the photograph.

Thicken a little of the white icing with sifted icing sugar and fill a plain forcing bag. Cut the bag so that it has a small slanting point and use this to pipe leaves between the flowers; hold the bag at an angle to the surface of the cake, press with the thumb and then lift forcing bag away with a slight pull (8).

To assemble the cake : lift the lower tier on to a cake stand. Place a 3-inch pillar in each of the circles of fowers. Carefully place the second tier on the pillars and arrange flowers, or chosen decoration, on the top.

105

Honey cake

½ lb honey
4 fl oz black coffee
1 tablespoon brandy
2 eggs
4 oz soft brown sugar
2 tablespoons oil
7 oz plain flour
3 teaspoons baking powder
1 teaspoon bicarbonate of soda
½ teaspoon cinnamon
½ teaspoon ginger
½ teaspoon mixed spice
½ teaspoon grated nutmeg
1 oz almonds (blanched and
   chopped — see page 154)
1 oz candied peel (chopped)
½ oz raisins (chopped)
½ oz sultanas (chopped)
½ oz dates (chopped)

Two loaf tins about 7½ by 3½ inches

This cake is eaten at Jewish New Year celebrations.

Method
Set oven at 325°F or Mark 3. Line tins with greaseproof paper.

Mix honey and coffee in a small pan and bring to the boil. Add brandy, then allow to cool. Beat eggs lightly in a mixing bowl and stir in the sugar and oil.

Sift the dry ingredients and mix in nuts and fruit. Stir flour and honey mixtures alternately into the egg mixture until the flour is combined. Quickly divide mixture between tins.

Bake in the pre-set oven for 30 minutes, then reduce heat to 300°F or Mark 2 and cook for 40-45 minutes more. The cake is done when it springs back immediately at the light touch of a finger.

Seal in an airtight tin and leave for two days before cutting.

Christmas chocolate log

1 plain, or chocolate-flavoured,
   swiss roll (see pages 126-128)
8-12 oz butter cream (see page 152)
   — flavoured with melted chocolate

For meringue suisse
1 egg white
2 oz caster sugar
little icing sugar
little chocolate (grated)

For decoration
6 oz boiled marzipan (see page 108)
little instant coffee (optional)
green colouring
little icing sugar

Forcing bag and 6-cut vegetable rose pipe

Method
Make the swiss roll; if making a plain one spread it with a little apricot jam before rolling it up. If making a chocolate one, however, spread it with chocolate butter cream when it has cooled a little and then roll up. The chocolate roll will give a much richer cake.

Make the meringue mixture and shape into mushrooms (see page 108). Dust the finished mushrooms with icing sugar and grated chocolate before baking.

Make boiled marzipan. Take two-thirds of this and make into small rounds to represent knots in the wood, and form the two ends of the log. If wished these can be coloured with a little instant coffee. Colour the remaining boiled marzipan with green colouring and roll it out. Shape and cut it to represent a trail of ivy.

When ready to decorate the log, trim the swiss roll and spread with a light coating of chocolate butter cream. Then place the two almond paste ends on the log. Pipe the remaining butter icing on to the log, placing the almond paste knots along it. Put the trail of ivy over and along the log and arrange the small meringue mushrooms around the side.

Sprinkle the top of the cake with icing sugar to give the effect of snow.

1

2

Christmas chocolate log with almond paste 'knots' and ends

1 *Forming the coffee-coloured almond paste into knots and ends for the Christmas chocolate log*
2 *Making a trail of ivy leaves from green-coloured almond paste*

More cake decorations

Attractive cake decorations can be made with almond paste. This recipe for boiled marzipan is the best to use as it is almost white and colours well. For other suggestions for shapes, see pages 107, 113.

Boiled marzipan

1 lb granulated sugar
6 fl oz and 1 teaspoon water
¾ lb ground almonds
2 egg whites (lightly beaten)
juice of ½ lemon
1 teaspoon orange flower water
3-4 tablespoons icing sugar

Curling a petal round a cone-shaped base of boiled marzipan. Use 2-3 petals only to make a bud

Method
Place the sugar and water in a saucepan and dissolve over gentle heat; bring it to the boil and cook steadily to 240°F. Remove the pan from the heat and beat the syrup until it looks a little cloudy, stir in the ground almonds, add the egg whites and cook over a gentle heat for 2-3 minutes. Add the flavourings and turn on to a marble slab or laminated surface dusted with icing sugar.

When the marzipan is cool, knead it until quite smooth. Colour and shape as required.

To make marzipan flowers
Divide the cool marzipan in half, colour one piece pale pink, the other a deeper pink. Roll both out thinly and cut into rounds with a 1-inch diameter plain cutter. Make a number of cone-shaped bases and curl the prepared petals round them. Build up with 2-3 petals for buds, or 5-6 petals for full-blown roses, mixing the shades of pink.

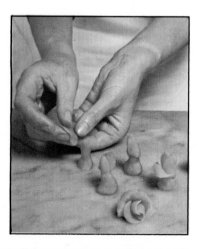

Building up the marzipan petals to form decorative flower heads. Use 5-6 petals for a full-blown rose

Meringue mushrooms

2 egg whites
4 oz caster sugar
1 oz plain block chocolate (finely grated)
little butter cream (see page 152)

Method

Set oven at 275°F or Mark 1.

Beat egg whites until stiff, whisk in 2 teaspoons of the measured sugar for 1 minute only. Fold in remaining sugar quickly and lightly with a metal spoon. Shape or pipe several small mushroom caps and stalks on an oiled and floured baking sheet. Dust caps with grated chocolate and bake in pre-set oven for about 45 minutes.

When meringues are cool, gently press a dent in underside of each cap, pipe in a little butter cream and fix in stalk.

How to make a paper piping cone

1 First take a 10-inch square of greaseproof paper, fold and cut into two triangles. Holding one of these with the right-angled (centre) point uppermost, fold the right-hand acute point over to meet the right-angled point

2 Next take the left-hand acute point and bring it right over and round to the back until all the points of the paper meet at the back to form cone or bag

3 Tuck over the flap formed where all the points meet the top of the cone. Crease this firmly to prevent cone from unfolding

4 Cut a little bit off the point of the cone, drop in the piping nozzle to see if it fits, and cut off a further amount if necessary. To start piping, drop nozzle into the bottom of the paper cone and fill with icing. Before using fold over the top of cone so that it presses on icing

Simple icing flowers

1 *Before starting any decoration, practise the shapes. If you want to decorate a cake with flowers, first practise making the centres of the flowers by building up a number of small circles, one on top of the other*

2 *Make a new piping cone and cut a small 'V' at the point. Practise making petals by pushing icing through the cone on to a firm surface and then drawing cone away quickly to make a sharp point*

3 *For finished flowers, use non-stick (silicone) kitchen paper as a base. (Black paper is only used for demonstrating the method.) Pipe on petals for outside of flowers, then pipe inside a second row of petals*

4 *Pipe centres, leave completed flowers on paper until dry. Then carefully lever flowers off with point of knife ; secure on cake with icing. With experience, flowers can be piped straight on to cake*

Simnel cake

8 oz plain flour
large pinch of salt
large pinch of baking powder
2 oz rice flour
8 oz sultanas (cleaned)
4 oz currants (cleaned)
4 oz glacé cherries (halved)
1 oz candied peel (finely chopped)
8 oz butter
grated rind of 2 lemons
8 oz caster sugar
4 eggs (separated)
beaten egg (to decorate)
3-4 tablespoons warm glacé, or
    fondant, icing (to decorate) —
    see pages 97 and 153

For almond paste
8 oz ground almonds
10 oz caster sugar
6 oz icing sugar (sifted)
2 egg yolks, or 1 whole egg
juice of $\frac{1}{2}$ lemon
$\frac{1}{2}$ teaspoon vanilla essence
$\frac{1}{4}$ teaspoon almond essence
1-2 teaspoons orange flower
    water

8-inch diameter cake tin

This Lancashire rich fruit cake was traditionally made for Mothering Sunday, but it is now also made for Easter.

Method

First make the almond paste : place the almonds, caster sugar and sifted icing sugar in a bowl and mix them together. Whisk egg yolks (or whole egg) with the lemon juice and flavourings and add this to the mixture of ground almonds and sugar. Pound paste lightly to release a little of the oil from the almonds. Knead paste with the hands until smooth. Store in greaseproof paper in a cool place until wanted.

Prepare the cake tin and set the oven at 350°F or Mark 4.

Sift the flour with the salt, baking powder and rice flour into a large basin. Mix together the prepared sultanas, currants, cherries and peel. Cream the butter with the lemon rind until soft, add the sugar and continue creaming until mixture is light and fluffy, then beat in the egg yolks. Whip egg whites until stiff.

Fold one-third of the flour into the mixture, then fold in the egg whites alternately with remaining flour and fruit. Put half the mixture into prepared tin, spreading it a little up the sides.

Take just over one-third of the almond paste, roll it into a smooth round, place it in the tin and cover with the remaining cake mixture. Bake in the pre-set oven for 2 hours, then reduce heat to 300°F or Mark 2 ; cover cake with a double thickness of non-stick (silicone) kitchen paper and continue cooking for about 30 minutes, or until a skewer inserted in the cake comes out clean. Allow the cake to cool a little, then remove it from the tin and slide it on to a baking sheet.

Decoration for Mothering Sunday

Divide the remaining almond paste in two, shape one portion into a number of even-sized balls and arrange them round the top edge of the cake. Brush the paste with a little beaten egg ; tie a band of greaseproof paper round the sides of the cake to hold the almond paste balls in position and put the cake in the oven (at 360-370°F or Mark 4-5) for a few minutes to brown. When the cake is cold, remove the greaseproof paper and pour a little warm glacé, or fondant, icing on the centre of the cake. Arrange a group of marzipan fruits, made from the last portion of almond paste (or boiled marzipan), on the icing and tie a ribbon round the cake.

Marzipan fruits

A wide variety of fruits can be made most successfully if you keep the shape and relative size of the different fruits in your mind's eye. The remaining almond paste can be used, but for perfection use the recipe for boiled marzipan (see page 108) as this is made with the whites of the eggs only and consequently it is easier to obtain the true colours of the fruits. Colour only a small piece at a time, adding the liquid colouring from the point of a skewer or teaspoon. Mould the fruits with the fingers, colour them and leave to harden before arranging them on the cake.

Simnel cake, decorated with icing and marzipan fruits for Mothering Sundy. For Easter, make one or two yellow chicks and some small eggs

Maypole birthday cake

For Victoria sandwich
6 oz butter
grated rind and juice of 1 medium-size orange
6 oz caster sugar
3 eggs (separated)
6 oz self-raising flour
pinch of salt

apricot glaze (see page 152)
glacé icing (made with 1 lb icing sugar, 3 rounded tablespoons granulated sugar, ¼ pint water and few drops pink colouring — see method, page 97)
royal icing (made with 5-6 oz icing sugar, 1 egg white, mauve and yellow colourings — see method, page 97)

8-9 inch diameter sandwich tin
One ½-inch dowel rod (12 inches long)
1 yard each narrow ribbon in four colours
Few artificial flowers wired together

Method

Grease and flour sandwich tin. Set oven at 375°F or Mark 5.

Soften the butter with the grated rind of the orange in a bowl. Add sugar and beat until light and fluffy. Add the egg yolks one at a time and beat again. Sift flour and salt into a bowl ; whisk egg whites until stiff. Fold flour and the strained juice of half the orange into the butter mixture, then fold in the egg whites. Turn at once into the prepared tin and bake in pre-set oven for about 40-45 minutes. Cool on a wire rack.

Brush cake with hot apricot glaze and leave to set.

Watchpoint This coating of glaze is to prevent cake crumbs spoiling the appearance of the icing when this is poured and spread over the cake.

Make the glacé icing, adding the strained juice of the second half of the orange to the sugar syrup and colouring the icing a pale shade of pink. Spread icing over the cake.

Make the royal icing for decoration. Colour it in two or three pastel shades and shape or pipe small flowers around the top and bottom edge of the cake. Pipe child's name and age on top.

To make the maypole : twist the ribbons round and up the rod and secure with a dab of glue or adhesive tape, letting the ends fall from the wreath of flowers which is fixed firmly to the top. Place the maypole in the centre of the cake and let the ribbons fall on to the table and lead to a name card.

Numeral birthday cake

This makes an original children's birthday cake. Frames in the shape of numerals 1 to 9 (and 0) can be bought at large stores.

Method

Bake your Victoria sandwich mixture, as given in the Maypole cake recipe (see page 114) in the correct numeral frame for the child's age. When cool place cake on a board ready for icing ; brush well with hot apricot glaze (see page 152) and leave until cold. Cover with glacé icing (see page 97), decorate with child's name and candles.

A numeral 7 shape is easy to prepare without a special frame. Bake a Victoria sandwich mixture in the usual way in an 8-inch square tin. When cold, cut cake in two strips, 8 inches by 4 inches, and trim the ends. Fit together in the shape of a 7. Glaze, ice, decorate.

Whisked sponges

Whisked sponges are the lightest of all cakes. They contain only a small proportion of flour and their texture depends almost entirely on the amount of air beaten in with the eggs.

The mixture is delicate and it is important that there should be no delays in mixing and baking, so remember that preparation plays a big part in the success of the finished cake.

Choice of ingredients Sponge cakes should be made with the finest ingredients to help their keeping qualities.

Eggs are best used when about three days old and give more volume if beaten when at room temperature.

Use caster sugar which is quite free of lumps. Granulated sugar is too coarse and does not dissolve completely when beaten with the eggs. If sugar is not dissolved, the finished cakes will have a speckly surface.

Flour should be plain and as fine as possible. It helps to dry the flour gently in the oven and sift it at least three times.

Finally, check recipe and weigh ingredients for even results.

Mixing Make sure that your mixing bowl, or pudding basin, and whisk are free from grease.

If mixing with a balloon whisk, use a mixing bowl. Gentle heat is needed to get the greatest volume from the eggs and at the same time to dissolve the sugar.

If using an electric or rotary beater, use a large pudding basin. In this case heat is not necessary. Whichever method you use, it is essential to get as much air as possible beaten into the mixture.

The cake batter is ready when a little lifted on the whisk falls in a thick ribbon on the mixture in the bowl and holds its shape.

Having beaten the sponge mixture so well, take care not to lose any of the air in it when adding the flour. Remove the whisk, sift the flour over the surface of the batter and cut and fold it in with a metal spoon. Mix in only enough to give a smooth mixture. Pour at once into the prepared tins and bake immediately.

117

Preparation of cake tins
Sponge cakes should have a firm, sugary casing, so brush or wipe the tins with a little melted or creamed shortening, taking particular care to reach the corners. Pour a little caster sugar in the tin, shake it well to coat the sides, then tip it out. Tap the tin to remove any surplus and then repeat the process with a little sifted flour.

Preparing the oven Set the oven at the correct temperature according to the recipe and arrange the shelves so that the cake will be in the centre of the oven. This will ensure that the cake has constant heat so that it bakes evenly.

Baking temperatures

Type of whisked sponge	Electric and solid fuel	Gas Mark
Sponge cake, fingers and drops	350-375°F	4-5
Swiss roll	325-375°F	3-5

Utensils

1 Swiss roll tin
2 Bun pan
3 Cake tin with removeable
   bottom
4 Savarin mould
5 Spring-form cake tin
6 Sponge finger pan

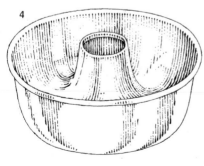

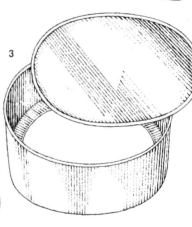

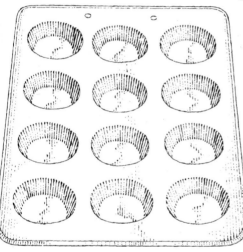

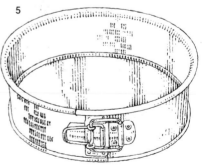

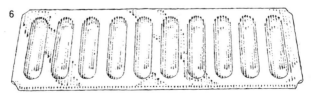

Sponge cake 1

3 oz plain flour
pinch of salt
3 eggs
4 ½ oz caster sugar

8-inch diameter cake tin

A soft sponge which keeps well and is suitable for filling with cream and serving with fruit.

Method
Set oven at 375°F or Mark 5 and prepare cake tin.

Have ready a large pan, half full of boiling water, over which the mixing bowl will rest comfortably without touching the water.

Sift the flour and salt well.

Break eggs into mixing bowl and beat in the sugar gradually. Remove the pan from the heat, place the bowl on top and whisk the eggs and sugar together until thick and mousse-like. This will take at least 5 minutes and the mixture will increase in volume and lighten in colour. When dropped from whisk it will make a 'ribbon' on itself. Remove bowl from pan of hot water and continue whisking until mixture is cold (a further 3-4 minutes).

Using a metal spoon, cut and fold the flour into the mixture. Put the mixture into the tin and bake in pre-set oven for 20-25 minutes until risen and brown. Turn out and cool on a rack.

Sponge cake 2

3 oz plain flour
pinch of salt
2 eggs
4 oz caster sugar

7 ½ -inch diameter savarin mould, or 7-inch diameter cake tin

A firm, dry sponge, suitable for soaking with fruit juice or serving with butter cream.

Method
Set the oven at 375°F or Mark 5 and prepare the savarin mould or cake tin.

Prepare the batter as for sponge cake 1. Bake in pre-set oven for 20-30 minutes until risen and brown. Turn out and cool on a rack.

Sponge cake 3

6 oz plain flour
pinch of salt
8 oz lump sugar
¾ teacup water
2 whole eggs
2 egg yolks
grated rind of 1 lemon

9-inch diameter cake tin

This cake keeps well and is excellent for icing, being firm and smooth when baked.

Method
Set the oven at 350°F or Mark 4 and prepare cake tin.

Sift the flour and salt well. Place the sugar and water in a pan and dissolve sugar over gentle heat. Boil steadily to the 'short thread' stage (218°F), pour it immediately on to the eggs and extra yolks and whisk to a thick mousse. Add the lemon rind.

Using a metal spoon, cut and fold the flour carefully into the batter. Turn it into the prepared tin and bake in the pre-set oven for about 1 hour. Lower heat after the first 30 minutes if cake is getting too brown. Turn out and cool on a rack.

Biscuit milanaise

2 oz plain flour
2 oz fécule (potato flour), or arrowroot
pinch of salt
4 eggs (2 separated)
8 oz caster sugar
grated rind of 1 lemon
1 oz currants (cleaned)

7½ -8 inch diameter cake tin

Method
Set the oven at 350°F or Mark 4 and prepare tin.

Sift flours and salt well together. Put 2 whole eggs and 2 egg yolks into a mixing bowl, add the sugar gradually and whisk it over gentle heat until thick and white (about 15 minutes).

Whisk the 2 egg whites until stiff and, using a metal spoon, fold into the mixture with the sifted flours, grated lemon rind and the currants.

Put in the prepared tin and bake in pre-set oven for about 1 hour. Lower heat after the first 30 minutes if cake is getting too brown. Turn out and cool.

Crusty top sponge

5 oz plain flour
pinch of salt
4 eggs (separated)
8 oz caster sugar
1 dessertspoon orange flower
   water

8-inch diameter cake tin

Method
Set the oven at 350°F or Mark 4 and prepare tin.

Sift the flour and salt well. Place the yolks with half the sugar and the orange flower water in a bowl and beat with a heavy whisk or wooden spatula until thick and mousse-like.

Whip the egg whites until stiff ; add the remaining sugar, 1 tablespoon at a time, and continue whisking until the mixture stands in peaks. Then, using a metal spoon, fold egg whites carefully into the yolk mixture with the flour.

Pour the batter into the prepared tin and bake in the pre-set oven for about 45 minutes. Turn out and cool on a rack.

Sponge fingers

$3\frac{1}{2}$ oz plain flour
pinch of salt
3 eggs (separated)
$3\frac{1}{2}$ oz caster sugar
icing sugar (for dusting)

Baking sheet, or sponge finger pans for about 18 fingers ; forcing bag and $\frac{1}{2}$-inch plain éclair nozzle

Method
Line a baking sheet with greaseproof paper, brush with melted lard or oil and dust it with flour (sponge finger pans may be used if preferred). Set the oven at 350°F or Mark 4.

Sift the flour and salt well. Cream the egg yolks and sugar together with a wooden spoon until thick and pale in colour. Whisk the egg whites until stiff. Fold a third of the flour into the egg yolks very carefully and then add the egg whites and remaining flour. Do not stir more than is necessary.

Put mixture into forcing bag and shape into fingers $3\frac{1}{2}$ inches long or fill pans. Dust them well with icing sugar and tilt the sheet to remove any surplus sugar. Bake in the pre-set oven for about 12 minutes. Then leave to cool.

Sponge drops

2 ½ oz plain flour
pinch of salt
3 eggs (separated)
3 oz caster sugar
1 teaspoon orange flower water,
   or lemon juice
icing sugar (for dredging)

Forcing bag ; ½-inch plain éclair nozzle

This recipe makes about 24 sponge drops.

Method
Set the oven at 350°F or Mark 4 and grease and flour a baking sheet.

Sift the flour and salt well. Place the egg yolks in a basin, add the sugar gradually and cream them together with a wooden spoon or heavy whisk until very thick and light in colour. Add the orange flower water or lemon juice.

Whisk the egg whites until stiff and dry, add 1 teaspoon to the yolk mixture and then fold in the flour. Using a metal spoon, and with great care, cut and fold in the remaining egg white to the flour and yolks.

Put the mixture into a forcing bag and shape into drops about 1½ inches in diameter (or shape with teaspoons) on to the baking sheet. Dredge them with icing sugar and bake in the pre-set oven for about 15-20 minutes. Leave to cool.

Crusty top sponge cake, sponge drops and sponge fingers

Small sponge cakes

2 $\frac{1}{2}$ oz plain flour
pinch of salt
3 eggs
3 oz caster sugar (plus extra for
dredging)

8-12 small sponge cake tins

Method
Set oven at 350°F or Mark 4, grease and flour tins. Make mixture as for sponge cake 1 (see page 121) and put into greased and floured tins. Dredge the top of each cake with caster sugar and bake in the pre-set oven for about 20 minutes. Leave to cool.

Flavourings for sponge cakes

Orange flower water, obtainable at a chemist, is the traditional flavouring for sponge cakes.

Alternatively grated lemon or orange rind can be used but do not overdo it. The grated rind of $\frac{1}{2}$ a small orange or lemon is quite enough ; too much will result in a sticky sponge.

Another way of flavouring is to place 2-3 leaves of sweet (rose) geranium or lemon verbena leaves on the bottom of the prepared cake tin before pouring in the mixture. This gives a delicious flavour to a plain sponge cake.

Swiss roll 1

2 oz plain flour
$\frac{1}{2}$ teaspoon baking powder
pinch of salt
2 eggs (beaten)
4 oz caster sugar
2 tablespoons water
2-3 drops of vanilla essence
icing, or caster, sugar (for
dusting)

For filling
3 tablespoons warm jam

Swiss roll tin, or paper case (see page 128), 8 inches by 12 inches

Method
Set the oven at 375°F or Mark 5 ; grease and flour swiss roll tin or paper case.

Sift the flour well with baking powder and salt. Beat the eggs with a whisk until thick, add the sugar gradually and continue beating until white.

Stir in the water and vanilla essence and add the flour to the mixture all at once. Beat with the whisk until just smooth and turn at once into the prepared tin or paper case. Spread it evenly and bake in pre-set oven for 12-15 minutes.

To turn out the cake : loosen the edges and turn immediately on to a tea towel or sheet of greaseproof paper, dusted with icing or caster sugar. Quickly and carefully remove the paper case (if used), trim the side edges of the swiss roll with a knife and spread with the warm jam. Roll the cake up at once and leave it to cool in the towel. Sprinkle liberally with sugar before serving.

Swiss roll 2

2 **oz plain flour**
1 **dessertspoon cornflour**
½ **teaspoon baking powder**
pinch of salt
4 **oz caster sugar**
2 **eggs (separated)**
1 **dessertspoon orange flower**
  water
icing, or caster, sugar (for dusting)

For filling
3 **tablespoons warm jam**

Swiss roll tin, or paper case (see page 128), 8 inches by 12 inches

This sponge rises well and has a thick spongy texture.

Method

Set the oven at 350 °F or Mark 4 ; grease and flour swiss roll tin or paper case.

Sift the flour with the cornflour, baking powder and salt four times. Set aside 2 tablespoons sugar ready to be added to the egg whites. Whisk the egg yolks until thick, adding a large portion of remaining sugar, then the orange flower water gradually, with rest of the caster sugar.

Whisk the egg whites until stiff, add the 2 tablespoons of reserved sugar and continue whisking until the mixture stands in peaks. Fold the whites into the yolks and lastly fold in the flour. Pour mixture into prepared tin or paper case, spread it evenly and bake in the pre-set oven for about 12 minutes.

Turn the cake at once on to a sugared tea towel and remove the paper case very quickly (if used). Trim edges with a knife, spread cake with warm jam and roll up quickly. Sprinkle with sugar before serving.

The paper case is torn away in two pieces, quickly and carefully, from the cooked swiss roll

Sides of swiss roll sponge are trimmed to give a neat edge and to remove the browned parts

After filling has been spread on, sponge is rolled up by gently tilting the paper, or tea towel

Chocolate swiss roll

1 oz plain flour
1 dessertspoon cocoa
pinch of salt
3 eggs (separated)
large pinch of cream of tartar
4 oz caster sugar
2-3 drops of vanilla essence
icing sugar (for dusting)

For filling
icing sugar
Chantilly cream, or coffee butter cream (see page 152)

Swiss roll tin, or paper case, 8 inches by 12 inches

Method

Set oven at 325°F or Mark 3 ; grease and flour swiss roll tin or paper case.

Sift the flour well with cocoa and salt. Separate the eggs and whisk the whites with the cream of tartar until stiff ; then gradually beat in half the sugar. Continue whisking until the mixture looks very glossy and will stand in peaks.

Cream the egg yolks until thick, then beat in the remaining sugar and add the vanilla essence. Stir the flour into the yolks and pour this mixture over the whites. Using a metal spoon, cut and fold carefully until thoroughly blended.

Turn the mixture into the prepared tin or paper case, bake in the pre-set oven for 20-25 minutes. Turn at once on to a sugared tea towel, trim the cake's edges and roll it up, with the towel inside the cake.

When cool, unroll cake carefully and fill with the chosen cream ; roll up again and dust with icing sugar before serving.

To make a swiss roll paper case

A paper case can be used instead of a tin for baking a swiss roll.

Choose a thick grease-proof paper or non-stick (silicone) kitchen paper.

Take a piece 1-2 inches larger than the size you require, for example 14 inches by 10 inches. Fold over the ends and sides to form a border of about $1\frac{1}{2}$ inches. Cut a slit at each corner and fold one cut piece over the other to mitre the corner. Fasten each corner with a paper clip so borders stand up. Slide case on to a baking sheet.

Chantilly cream

Whip a $\frac{1}{4}$-pint carton of double cream until just thickening ; then add 1 teaspoon caster sugar and 2-3 drops of vanilla essence. Then continue beating until the cream holds its shape. (In warm weather and in a warm kitchen, if the sugar and essence are added before first whisking, it prevents cream getting thick.)

American cakes

America has a wonderful selection of recipes for cakes and cookies, stemming from all over the world. Many were taken there by early settlers and have become established over the years as traditional favourites.

Also included in this section are some typically American frostings and icings.

Don't forget that American measures are different from ours, and they also have several grades of flour from which to choose for different recipes. Our recipes are the nearest British equivalents, using the finest white flour available.

Brownies

*2 oz unsweetened chocolate
2½ oz shortening
2 eggs
8 oz caster sugar
3 oz plain flour
½ teaspoon baking powder
pinch of salt
4 oz shelled walnuts (roughly
   chopped)

8-inch square cake tin

Method
Set the oven at 350°F or Mark 4.

Cut up or grate the chocolate, put in a saucepan with the shortening and melt over gentle heat. Whisk the eggs and sugar together until light, add the chocolate mixture. Sift the flour with the baking powder and salt and stir into mixture with a wooden spoon ; stir in the nuts.

Spread into the prepared tin and bake for 30-35 minutes in the pre-set oven, or until a 'dull' crust has formed. Allow to cool slightly and cut into squares.

*If you can't get unsweetened chocolate, mix 2 oz cocoa with 5 tablespoons water and cook to a cream, and increase the quantity of shortening to 3 oz.

Angel cake

2 oz plain flour
6½ oz caster sugar
6 egg whites
pinch of salt
¾ teaspoon cream of tartar
3 drops of vanilla essence
2 drops of almond essence

8-9 inch diameter angel cake tin (with funnelled base)

This should be made with the finest flour available and it is possible to buy special flour. But it can be made with any good plain white flour if first sifted 3-4 times through a fine nylon strainer.

Method
Set oven at 375°F or Mark 5. Sift the flour and 3½ oz caster sugar three times and set on one side. Place the egg whites, salt and cream of tartar in a large, dry basin and whisk with a rotary beater until foamy.

Add the remaining sugar, 2 tablespoons at a time, and the essences and continue beating until the mixture will stand in peaks. Carefully fold in the sifted flour and sugar. Turn the mixture into the clean, dry tin, level the surface and draw a knife through to break any air bubbles. Bake the cake in the pre-set oven for 30-35 minutes or until no imprint remains when your finger lightly touches the top.

When cake is ready, turn it upside down on a wire rack and leave until quite cold, when the cake will fall easily from the tin.

Serve plain for tea or with fruit for a lunch party. Pull into pieces with two forks rather than cut with a knife as the texture is very delicate.

Angel cake Waldorf

2 oz plain flour
6½ oz caster sugar
6 egg whites
pinch of salt
¾ teaspoon cream of tartar
3 drops of vanilla essence
2 drops of almond essence

For filling
3-4 oz plain block chocolate
1-2 tablespoons water
½ pint double cream
1 dessertspoon caster sugar

8-9 inch diameter angel cake tin
(with funnelled base)

Method

Prepare angel cake (see method, page 131).

To prepare the filling : melt the chocolate in the water, then allow to cool. Whip the cream until thick, add the sugar and chocolate and continue whisking until it stands in peaks. Chill.

Place the cake upside down on a plate or waxed paper. Slice a 1-inch layer off the top of the cake and put this top lid on one side. Cut down and around the inside of the cake 1 inch from the outer edge and 1 inch from the centre hole, leaving a wall of cake about 1 inch thick and a base of 1 inch at the bottom. Remove this middle 'ring' with a spoon (it can be discarded) ; set cake on serving plate. Completely fill the cavity with the chilled filling, replace 'lid' of cake and press gently. Serve a bowl of sugared raspberries or strawberries separately.

Drawing a knife through the cake mixture to break up any air bubbles

Apple sauce cake

8 oz plain flour
1 teaspoon baking powder
$\frac{1}{4}$ teaspoon ground cinnamon
$\frac{1}{4}$ teaspoon ground nutmeg
$\frac{1}{4}$ teaspoon mixed spice
1 teaspoon salt
3 oz shortening
11 oz caster sugar
1 egg
$\frac{3}{4}$ cup canned apple sauce
1$\frac{1}{2}$ oz walnuts (roughly chopped)
4 oz seeded raisins
icing sugar (for dusting)

8-9 inch square cake tin

Method
Set oven at 350°F or Mark 4 and grease the cake tin.

Sift the flour with the baking powder, spices and salt and set on one side. Cream the shortening and sugar together, add the egg and beat well. Stir in the apple sauce and then fold in the flour, walnuts and raisins. Turn the mixture into the prepared tin and bake in pre-set oven for about 45 minutes.

When cool, dust the top with icing sugar.

The cakes on this page are usually served with coffee at lunchtime. Their texture is certainly more like our sponge puddings.

Upside-down cake

2$\frac{1}{2}$ oz butter
2$\frac{1}{2}$ oz brown sugar

9 oz plain flour
4 teaspoons baking powder
$\frac{1}{2}$ teaspoon salt
2 oz butter, or margarine, or shortening
5 oz caster sugar
1 egg (well whisked)
$\frac{1}{4}$ pint milk

To decorate
cooked, or canned, fruit (slices of pineapple and cherries, or prunes — drained)
glacé cherries, or walnuts

8$\frac{1}{2}$-9 inch diameter layer cake tin (with sloping sides)

Method
Cream the 2$\frac{1}{2}$ oz butter with the brown sugar and spread mixture over the bottom and sides of the prepared tin.

Arrange the drained fruit over the butter-sugar coating and decorate with the glacé cherries or walnuts.

Set the oven at 350°F or Mark 4. Sift the flour with the baking powder and salt and set aside. Soften the 2 oz butter, or fat, with a wooden spoon ; add the sugar and well whisked egg and beat thoroughly until light and fluffy. Stir in the flour alternately with the milk.

Spoon cake mixture into the prepared tin and bake in the pre-set oven for 50-60 minutes. When the cake is ready (test with fine skewer or trussing needle), invert it immediately on to the serving plate. Leave for a few minutes for the brown sugar mixture to run down over the cake, then remove cake tin.

Walnut layer cake

9 oz plain flour
3 teaspoons baking powder
½ teaspoon salt
6 oz shortening
12 oz caster sugar
7½ fl oz milk
4 drops of vanilla essence
4 egg whites
American frosting (see page 136)
3 tablespoons chopped walnuts
8 walnut halves (to decorate)

Three 8-inch diameter sandwich tins

Method
Set the oven at 350°F or Mark 4.

Sift the flour with the baking powder and salt and set on one side. Beat the shortening and sugar together until very light and soft. Stir in the flour alternately with the milk and flavouring, and lastly fold in the stiffly-whisked egg whites.

Divide the mixture evenly between the prepared tins, smooth the top with a palette knife and bake for 30-35 minutes in the pre-set oven. Test with a fine skewer or trussing needle.

When the cake is cool prepare the American frosting to use as filling and topping. Take 4 tablespoons of this frosting, mix with the chopped walnuts and quickly spread between the layers. Cover the top and sides of the cake with the remaining frosting and decorate with the walnut halves.

Cherry layer cake

Follow the recipe for walnut layer cake (left), and divide the mixture as before into three, but colour one portion a delicate pink with a few drops of liquid carmine. Fill into three 8-inch diameter prepared tins, bake and allow to cool.

Prepare the American frosting but reserve one-third of the mixture and into this fold 1 small bottle of maraschino cherries, drained and halved. Sandwich the layers together with this filling, having the pink cake in the middle, and then cover the top and sides with the remaining frosting.

Pineapple layer cake

Follow the recipe for walnut layer cake (left), bake and allow it to cool. Prepare the same quantity of American frosting but take 3 tablespoons of it, mix with 3 tablespoons of drained, chopped pineapple and spread between the layers. Cover the top and sides with the remaining frosting and decorate with slices of candied pineapple.

Right : Walnut layer cake

American frosting

1 lb lump sugar
¾ cup water
pinch of cream of tartar
2 egg whites
3-4 drops of vanilla essence
sugar thermometer

Method
Put sugar and water in a sauce-pan over a low heat and dissolve without stirring. Add the cream of tartar (in 1 teaspoon of water), put on the lid and bring to the boil. After 2 minutes remove the lid, put in a sugar thermometer and boil sugar syrup steadily to 240°F.

Meanwhile whisk the egg whites until stiff.

When sugar syrup reaches required temperature, stop the boiling by dipping the bottom of the pan in cold water. Then, holding the pan well above the bowl of egg whites, pour in the hot syrup in a thin steady stream, whisking all the time. Continue beating until the mixture loses its satiny appearance and will hold its shape. Add vanilla essence. Spread frosting quickly over the cake with a palette knife in bold sweeping strokes, as at this stage the icing sets quickly.

Note : it is possible to make this frosting without a sugar thermometer. After boiling for 8 minutes, test in the following way. Take a small kitchen tool (such as a whisk) that has a rigid ring or loop at the end, dip this ring into the boiling syrup and then, holding it aloft, blow through the ring ; if the syrup is ready it flies away like a feather or bubble.

Chocolate fudge icing

1 lb granulated sugar
½ pint water
1 tablespoon golden syrup
2 oz unsalted butter
2 oz cocoa

Sugar thermometer

Method
Place all the ingredients in a large saucepan, blend together and dissolve the sugar over gentle heat. Bring to the boil and cook to 238°F on the sugar boiling thermometer — this is known as the soft-ball stage.

Watchpoint To prevent possible sticking, draw a wooden spoon through the mixture from time to time, but never stir continually as this can cause the icing to 'grain' (go sugary).

Remove the pan from the heat, leave the mixture until cool, then beat with a wooden spoon until thick enough to hold its shape.

Caramel icing

5 tablespoons creamy milk
3 oz butter
2 tablespoons caster sugar
12 oz icing sugar (sifted)

Method
Heat the milk and butter to-gether. Place the caster sugar in a small heavy saucepan and caramelise it over gentle heat. Add the milk and butter, stir-ring until the caramel is dis-solved.

Stir in the icing sugar and beat well until the icing is smooth, creamy and of a spreading consistency.

Caramel cake

12 oz caster sugar
$\frac{1}{2}$ teacup hot black coffee, or water
8$\frac{1}{2}$ oz plain flour
3 teaspoons baking powder
1 teaspoon salt
4 oz shortening
2 eggs (well beaten)

Two 9-inch diameter sandwich tins

Method
Set the oven at 350°F or Mark 4.

Place 4 oz of the caster sugar in a small, heavy saucepan, dissolve it over gentle heat without stirring and boil steadily to a rich brown caramel. Slowly add the hot coffee or water and stir over low heat until all the lumps are dissolved. Pour this mixture into a measure, leave to cool and add cold water to make 7$\frac{1}{2}$ fl oz.

Sift the flour with the baking powder and salt and set on one side. Soften the shortening with a wooden spoon and beat in the remaining sugar ; add the eggs, a little at a time, and beat thoroughly until light and fluffy. Stir in the flour alternately with the caramel mixture and then pour into the prepared tins. Bake in the pre-set oven for about 25-30 minutes or until cooked.

When the cake is cool, sandwich the halves, and coat, with caramel icing.

Banana cake

8 oz plain flour
1 teaspoon baking powder
$\frac{1}{4}$ teaspoon bicarbonate of soda
pinch of salt
4 oz shortening
12 oz caster sugar
2 large eggs (well beaten)
3 medium-size bananas (mashed)
4 tablespoons milk

To finish
$\frac{1}{2}$ pint double cream (whipped and sweetened)
2 bananas (sliced)
2 tablespoons icing sugar

Two 9-inch diameter sandwich tins

Method
Set oven at 350°F or Mark 4.

Sift the flour with the baking powder, bicarbonate of soda and salt ; set on one side.

Cream the shortening and sugar together until light and fluffy ; add the eggs gradually and beat thoroughly. Stir in the sifted flour alternately with the mashed bananas and milk ; pour into the prepared tins and bake in pre-set oven for about 30 minutes or until cake is cooked.

When cool, sandwich cake with the cream and sliced bananas and dust top with sifted icing sugar.

Coconut cake

7½ oz plain flour
2 teaspoons baking powder
½ teaspoon salt
4 oz shortening
9 oz caster sugar
2 large eggs (well beaten)
¼ pint milk
4 drops of vanilla essence
American frosting (see page 136)
4 oz desiccated coconut

Two 8-inch diameter sandwich tins

Method

Set the oven at 350°F or Mark 4.

Sift the flour with the baking powder and salt. Cream the shortening with the sugar until light and fluffy, add the well-beaten eggs, a little at a time, and beat them in very thoroughly. Stir in the sifted flour alternately with the milk and flavouring.

Pour the cake mixture into the prepared tins and bake for 25-30 minutes until cooked. Test cake with a fine skewer or trussing needle.

When cool, first sandwich with American frosting and then cover the top and sides. Before the icing sets, cover the cake thickly with the coconut.

Devil's food cake

6 oz plain flour
$\frac{1}{4}$ teaspoon baking powder
1 teaspoon bicarbonate of soda
pinch of salt
2 oz cocoa
$7\frac{1}{2}$ fl oz cold water
4 oz shortening
10 oz caster sugar
2 eggs
chocolate fudge icing (see page 136)

Two 8-inch diameter sandwich tins

Method
Set oven at 350°F or Mark 4.

Sift the flour with the baking powder, bicarbonate of soda and salt. Blend the cocoa with the water and set aside. Soften the shortening with a wooden spoon, add the sugar and beat until light and very soft.

Whisk the eggs until frothy, add to the shortening and sugar mixture a little at a time and beat well. Stir in the sifted flour alternately with the cocoa and water, divide the mixture between the two tins and bake in the pre-set oven for 30-35 minutes. Cake is ready when a fine skewer or trussing needle comes away clean. Leave to cool, then sandwich the halves, and cover the cake, with chocolate fudge icing.

Top : cocoa and water is stirred into devil's food cake mixture alternately with flour. Above : mixing ingredients for chocolate fudge icing while the cake is cooling

Devil's food cake continued

Devil's food cake is sandwiched, and covered, with chocolate fudge icing

Biscuits

Originally, biscuits were 'baked twice' to give them their crispness. This is not normal now, but with careful mixing of the dough, and if you take care to roll it thinly, the same effect can be achieved.

Don't expect home-baked biscuits to resemble in any way the types that are made commercially. Bought biscuits are for the most part cooked in special ovens and cannot be imitated at home. Instead, experiment with recipes that cannot be rivalled in the shops. Family and guests will be delighted.

Home-baked biscuits are best made in small quantities and eaten quickly. To store, keep them on their own (never mix with cakes) in an airtight tin, preferably sealed with a sheet of greaseproof paper under the lid. Let biscuits cool thoroughly before putting into tins so that there is no warm, moist air to collect in the tin, and do not let them stand once they are cool or they will start to gather fresh moisture from the air.

Except for iced ones, it is possible to crisp up soft biscuits by putting them in a moderate oven for a few minutes.

Florentines

3¾ oz butter
4 oz caster sugar
scant 1 oz glacé cherries
  (quartered)
3¾ oz almonds (blanched and finely
  chopped — see page 154)
1¼ oz almonds (blanched and flaked)
3½ candied orange peel
  (finely chopped)
2 tablespoons double cream
4 oz plain block chocolate, or
  chocolate couverture

Plain pastry cutter ; confectioner's comb

Method

Grease a baking sheet with a little melted lard.

Melt the butter in a pan, add the sugar and bring it slowly to the boil. Stir in the cherries, chopped and flaked almonds and candied peel. Whip the cream until it is thick, then fold it into the mixture ; leave it to cool and set. Set the oven at 350°F or Mark 4.

Drop the mixture in teaspoons on to the prepared baking sheet, leaving plenty of space between each one as the biscuits spread during cooking. Bake in the pre-set moderate oven for 5-7 minutes. After 4 minutes remove the baking sheet from the oven and pull together the edges of each biscuit with a plain pastry cutter. Return the biscuits to the oven to finish cooking. Then allow them to cool a little on the baking sheet before removing them with a thin, sharp knife.

Melt the chocolate on a plate over a pan of hot water, remove from the heat and allow it to cool to the consistency of a thick smooth paste, working well with a palette knife to keep it glossy. Dip or spread the smooth side of the biscuits with the prepared chocolate and, when it is on the point of setting, work it in wavy lines with a confectioner's comb (see photograph).

> **A confectioner's comb** is a flat piece of plastic with indentations, like a comb, at one side. This is drawn over melted chocolate, which is on the point of setting, to give a decorative wavy line. A substitute is an ordinary 'setting' comb.

Above : pulling biscuit edges together with cutter before final cooling
Below : working the chocolate in wavy lines with confectioner's comb

Amaretti secchi
(Dry macaroons)

3 ½ oz ground almonds (see page 154)
4 ½ oz caster sugar
1 ½ oz vanilla sugar (see page 155)
2 egg whites
2 tablespoons kirsch
3-4 almonds (split and shredded —
  see page 154)
icing sugar (for dusting)

Method
Set oven at 350°F or Mark 4.
Pound the almonds and both
kinds of sugar with 1 egg white.
Whip the second egg white until
stiff and fold it into the almond
mixture with the kirsch. Divide
the mixture into pieces the size
of a walnut, roll between the
palms of your hands and place
on a sheet of non-stick (silicone)
kitchen paper on a baking sheet
and cook in the pre-set oven
for 20-30 minutes. Place a shred
of almond on the top of each
macaroon and dust with a little
icing sugar.

Vanilla fork biscuits

4 oz butter
2 oz caster sugar
5 oz self-raising flour
2-3 drops of vanilla essence

Method
Set oven at 375°F or Mark 5-6.
  Soften the butter with a
wooden spoon, add the sugar,
and cream until white. Stir in
the flour and vanilla essence.
Roll the mixture into balls the
size of a walnut, place on a
greased baking sheet and
flatten with a fork. Bake in pre-
set oven for 7-8 minutes.

Iced chocolate biscuits

4 oz butter
2 oz caster sugar
4 oz self-raising flour
pinch of salt
1 oz sweetened chocolate
  powder

For glacé icing
1 lb icing sugar
½ egg white (optional)
pink and blue colouring (optional)

Method
Set oven at 375°F or Mark 5.
  Soften the butter in a bowl,
work in the sugar with a wooden
spoon and beat until light. Sift
flour with salt and chocolate
powder into a bowl, and stir into
the mixture. Roll into balls the
size of a small walnut, place
well apart on a greased baking
tray and flatten with a wet fork.
Bake for 8-10 minutes, leave
biscuits for 1-2 minutes on the
tin before lifting on to a wire
rack to cool.
  To make the glacé icing ; sift
just over half the icing sugar
into a basin and mix to a stiff
paste with a little water, adding
it 1 teaspoon at a time. Stand
the basin in a saucepan of hot
water and stir gently until the
icing thins a little. Coat each
biscuit with white icing and
leave to set.
  For a children's party, mix the
egg white with a fork, beat in
sufficient sifted icing sugar to
give a very stiff mixture ; divide
in two and colour one half pink
and the other blue. Pipe the
initials of each child on the
biscuits — pink for a girl, blue
for a boy. You'll be surprised
how quickly the biscuits
disappear.

144

Brandy snaps

4 oz butter
4 oz demerara sugar
4 oz golden syrup
4 oz plain flour
pinch of salt
1 teaspoon ground ginger
1 teaspoon lemon juice
2-3 drops of vanilla essence

This quantity makes about 20, and $\frac{1}{4}$ pint of double cream will fill 8-12 brandy snaps.

Method
Set the oven at 325°F or Mark 3. Put the butter, sugar and syrup into a saucepan and heat gently until the butter has melted and sugar dissolved. Leave to cool slightly. Sift flour with salt and ginger into mixture, stir well, adding lemon juice and vanilla essence.

Put teaspoons of mixture on a well-greased baking sheet at least 4 inches apart and cook in pre-set oven for 8 minutes. Leave biscuits for 2-3 minutes, then remove from the tin with a sharp knife, turn over and roll round the handle of a wooden spoon. Store in an airtight tin as soon as they are cold. Serve plain or filled with whipped cream.

Only a teaspoon of mixture should be put on the baking sheet ; leave room for expansion between each

Before the brandy snaps get too cold, turn them over and roll them up on the handle of a wooden spoon

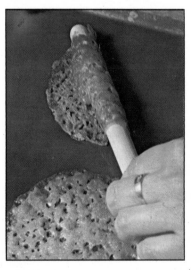

145

Cigarettes russes biscuits

2 egg whites
4 oz caster sugar
2 oz butter
2 oz plain flour (sifted)
2-3 drops of vanilla essence

These biscuits are one of the many varieties of little cakes and sweetmeats (known as petits gâteaux and petits fours) which may be served with dishes such as ices or mousses, or on their own.

Method
Break up the egg whites in a basin, add the sugar and beat with a fork until smooth. Melt the butter and add with the sifted flour to the mixture. Flavour with 2-3 drops of vanilla essence.

Spread the mixture in oblongs on the greased and floured baking sheet and bake for 5-6 minutes in an oven at 400°F or Mark 6. (It is a good idea to test the mixture by baking one only at first. If difficult to handle, add a pinch of flour, or if too firm and hard, you can add 1 dessertspoon of melted butter.)

Take the oblongs out of the oven and allow to stand for 1-2 seconds, then remove them with a sharp knife, placing them upside down on the table. Roll each one tightly round a wooden spoon handle, skewer or pencil, holding it firmly with your hand. Remove at once from the spoon, and allow to cool. Store in an airtight tin.

Gaufrettes viennoises

8 oz plain flour
pinch of salt
3 oz caster sugar
1 egg
3 oz ground almonds (see page 154)
6 oz butter

To decorate
a little royal icing
a little redcurrant jelly (see page 155)

Forcing bag, fine plain nozzle

Method
Set the oven at 375°F or Mark 5. Sift the flour with the salt on to your working surface, then make a well in the centre of the flour. Place the sugar and egg in this and sprinkle the almonds on the flour. Using your fingertips, mix the sugar and egg together until light and creamy, work in the butter and then gradually absorb the flour and almonds. Knead until paste is smooth and leave in a cool place for 30 minutes.

Roll out paste to an oblong, $\frac{1}{8}$ inch thick, place this on an ungreased baking sheet. Trim edges of the paste with a floured knife, then cut into 2-inch squares. Add a good pinch of flour to the royal icing, fill it into a forcing bag, and decorate half the squares with a lattice pattern. Bake paste in pre-set oven for about 7-8 minutes until a pale golden-brown. When cool, spread each plain square with redcurrant jelly and place a decorated square on top.

Galettes nantaises

4¼ oz plain flour
1¾ oz butter
2 oz caster sugar
1¾ oz ground almonds
salt
2 egg yolks

To finish
½ egg (beaten)
1 tablespoon ground almonds
caster sugar (for dredging)

2 ½-inch diameter fluted cutter

Nantes, in north-west France, is renowned for its biscuits.

Method
Set oven at 375°F or Mark 5 and lightly grease a baking sheet. Work the paste in the same way as for French flan pastry (see method page 154), working almonds in with the flour. Chill pastry for 1 hour in refrigerator, then roll it out fairly thinly and cut out into rounds with the cutter. Place rounds on prepared sheet and brush with beaten egg.

Mark the tops of the rounds into squares with the prongs of a fork, put a pinch of ground almonds in the centre of each one. Dredge with sugar and bake in pre-set oven for 7-8 minutes.

Duchesses pralinées

3 egg whites
3½ oz sugar
1 oz plain flour
1 oz ground almonds
1 oz ground hazelnuts (grilled)
1 oz butter (melted)

For filling
4 oz quantity of coffee butter cream (see page 152)

Method
Set oven at 275-325°F or Mark 2-3. Whip egg whites stiffly, fold in the sugar, flour, nuts and the melted butter. Spread biscuit out in ovals on a buttered and floured baking sheet, bake in pre-set oven until golden-brown. Lift ovals off on to a wire rack and when cool sandwich together (in pairs) with butter cream.

Galettes suisses

4¼ oz ground almonds
4¼ oz plain flour
4¼ oz sugar
1½ oz butter
3 egg yolks, or 1 egg
vanilla essence
salt

To finish
½ egg (beaten)
1 oz almonds (blanched and finely
  shredded — see page 154)
caster sugar (for dusting)

2½ -inch diameter fluted cutter

Method
Set oven at 350°F or Mark 4
and lightly grease a baking
sheet.

Prepare the biscuits in the
same way as for galettes nan-
taises (see page 147). Cut out
into rounds, place on prepared
baking sheet and brush with
beaten egg. Cover with the
almonds, dust with caster sugar
and bake in pre-set oven for
8-10 minutes.

Vénitiennes

4 oz quantity of, or trimmings of,
  French flan pastry (see page 154)
pinch of plain flour
5 oz quantity of royal icing
  (see page 97)
apricot glaze (see page 152)

Method
Set oven at 375°F or Mark 5.

Roll out the French flan
pastry thinly. Add flour to the
royal icing, spread it smoothly
over the pastry and, using a
floured knife, cut into 2-inch
squares.

Fill paper cornet with a little
reduced apricot glaze and
pipe a 'Union Jack' pattern on
to each biscuit. Place the
biscuits a little distance apart
(because they may spread
slightly in cooking) on an un-
greased baking sheet. Bake in
pre-set oven for 10-12 minutes.

*Galettes suisses and vénitiennes
cooling on a wire rack after baking*

148

Cheese sablés

3 oz cheese (grated)
3 oz plain flour (sifted)
3 oz butter
salt and pepper
1 egg (lightly beaten)

Sablé (sandy) describes a rich biscuit dough so named because of its short, crumbly texture

Method

Sift flour into a bowl. Cut butter into flour with a palette knife and, as soon as pieces are well coated with flour, rub in with your fingertips until mixture resembles fine breadcrumbs.

Add cheese and season to taste. Press mixture together to make a dough. Flour, wrap dough in greaseproof paper, chill in refrigerator. Set oven at 375°F or Mark 5.

Carefully roll out pastry into a fairly thin oblong, flouring rolling pin well because this pastry tends to stick ; if it does, ease it free with a palette knife. Cut into strips about 2 inches wide. Brush with beaten eg and cut strips into triangles.

Place sablés on a baking sheet lined with greaseproof paper, a d cook in the pre-set oven for 10 minutes until golden-brown.

Watchpoint Take baking sheet out of oven at once. Lift off greaseproof paper, with cooked sablés on it. Cheese scorches easily so that if you remove them from oven one by one, the last biscuits could become scorched through over-cooking.

Serve the sablés cold.

Hazelnut, or walnut, biscuits

4 oz hazelnuts, or 3 oz walnuts
4 oz butter
3 oz caster sugar
6 oz plain flour (sifted)

For filling
thick honey
icing sugar (for dusting)

2 ½-inch diameter plain cutter

This quantity makes 6-8 biscuits, when sandwiched.

Method
Toast the hazelnuts in the oven, then rub them in a coarse cloth to remove the skins. Grind them through a nut mill or cheese grater (or chop walnuts). Cream the butter, add sugar a little at a time and beat until fluffy. Then work in the flour, with the nuts, in two lots. When a paste is formed put it in the refrigerator for about 15-20 minutes. Set oven at 350 °F or Mark 4.

Roll out dough to about $\frac{1}{4}$ inch thick, stamp into rounds and prick lightly. Place rounds on a baking sheet and bake in the pre-set oven for 7-10 minutes. Take out of oven and cool slightly on the sheet before lifting off. When cool, sandwich biscuits with the honey. Dust with a little icing sugar.

Almond biscuits

3 oz butter
3 oz caster sugar
2 oz plain flour
pinch of salt
3 oz almonds (blanched and finely shredded) — see page 154

These biscuits are known as 'tuiles' because they resemble curved tiles. They are particularly good served with fresh fruit salad or fruit-flavoured mousses and soufflés.

Method
First, set the oven at 400°F or Mark 6. Soften butter, add sugar and beat well with wooden spoon until light and fluffy. Sift flour with a pinch of salt and stir into the mixture with the almonds. Put mixture a teaspoon at a time on to a well-greased baking tin and flatten with a wet fork.

Watchpoint Leave plenty of space between the biscuits because they will spread during cooking.

Bake in the oven until just coloured (6-8 minutes). Allow to stand a second or two before removing from the tin with a sharp knife. Curl on a rolling pin until set. Store when cool in an airtight container.

Appendix

Notes and basic recipes

Butter cream

2 oz granulated sugar
4 tablespoons water
2 egg yolks
6 oz unsalted butter
flavouring as required

Method
Dissolve the sugar in water in a saucepan over gentle heat, then boil it steadily until the syrup forms a slim 'thread' between the finger and thumb (216-218°F on a sugar thermometer).
Watchpoint To test between the finger and thumb, remove a little syrup from the pan, off the heat, with the handle of a teaspoon ; cool it and then test.

When bubbles subside, pour the syrup on to the egg yolks and whisk until mixture is thick and mousse-like. Cream the butter until soft and add the egg mousse gradually. Flavour to taste with melted sweetened chocolate or coffee essence or the zest of orange or lemon rind and use as required.

Custard sauce
(Crème à la vanille)

½ pint creamy milk
2 tablespoons caster sugar
2-3 drops of vanilla essence, or
    ½ vanilla pod (split)
2 egg yolks

Method
Put the milk in a pan, add the sugar with vanilla essence or, if using a vanilla pod, infuse it in milk for 10 minutes, keeping pan covered. Take out pod, then add sugar.

Cream the yolks in a bowl, bring the milk to scalding point and pour on gradually. Blend mixture together and return to the pan ; stir con-

tinually over a gentle heat with a wooden spatula or spoon. Stir gently to avoid splashing. When the custard coats the spoon and looks creamy, strain back into the bowl.

Dredge a little caster sugar over the top and leave to cool. This coating of sugar melts and helps prevent a skin forming.
Watchpoint Should the custard get too hot and begin to curdle, turn at once into the basin without straining and whisk briskly for 2-3 seconds. Remember that gentle heat helps to prevent a custard from curdling and makes it creamier.

Fruit glazes
Apricot glaze
This glaze can be made in fairly large quantities at a time, as it keeps well in a covered jar. It can be used with all yellow fruits.

To make 1 lb of glaze : turn 1 lb of apricot jam into a saucepan and add the juice from ½ a lemon and 4 tablespoons water. Bring slowly to the boil, then simmer for 5 minutes. If glaze is to be kept, strain, return to pan and boil for a further 5 minutes before cooling and putting into a jam jar.

If you want to use it immediately, continue boiling until the mixture is thick, then brush generously over the fruit. If using a smooth jam (with no lumps of fruit) water is not needed.

Redcurrant glaze
Homemade redcurrant jelly is best as it gives the right sharpness of flavour to the fresh fruit. Beat the jelly with a fork or small whisk until it liquefies, then rub through a strainer into a small saucepan. Heat gently without stirring until quite clear (boiling will spoil both colour and flavour). When brushing this glaze over the fruit use a very

soft brush. Always work from the centre outwards, drawing the brush, well laden with the glaze, towards the edge.

Icing
Colouring and flavouring icing
You should use edible colouring for icing. Take great care when adding a colour because one drop too many can change a subtle shading into a gaudy one. A skewer dipped in the bottle of colouring is the best method of adding a colour. From one bowl of icing, you can have five colour changes : from white to yellow, to pink or green, to coffee, to chocolate.

Flavourings are varied but are not meant to overpower and spoil the taste of the cake. You can buy several flavouring essences but you can also make them : strained orange or lemon fruit juice ; coffee powder dissolved in a little water ; melted chocolate, or cocoa blended with water.

To improve the whiteness of royal icing, add a tiny spot of blue colouring on the point of a skewer and beat it in very thoroughly ; too much blue gives icing a greyish tint. Also, 1-2 teaspoons of glycerine added to royal icing will prevent it from becoming excess-ively hard, and a squeeze of lemon juice added helps to counteract its sweetness.

Fondant icing

1 lb lump sugar
8 tablespoons water
pinch of cream of tartar

A sugar thermometer is essential for this recipe.

You can now buy blocks or packets of powder of fondant icing. Simply follow the manufacturer's instructions.

Method
Place the sugar and water in a saucepan and dissolve without stirring over a low heat. Using a brush dipped in cold water, wipe round pan at level of the syrup to prevent a crust forming. Add the cream of tartar (dis-solved in 1 teaspoon of water), place the lid on the pan, increase the heat and bring to the boil.

Remove the lid after 2 minutes, put a sugar thermometer in and boil the syrup steadily to 240°F. When it has reached this tempera-ture take the pan off the heat at once, wait for the bubbles to subside then pour the mixture very slowly on to a damp marble or laminated plastic slab. Work with a wooden spatula until it be-comes a firm and white fondant. Take a small piece of fondant at a time and knead with the fingertips until smooth.

For storing, pack fondant icing in an airtight jar or tin. When you want to use it, gently warm the fondant with a little sugar syrup to make a smooth cream. The icing should then flow easily. Flavour and colour it just before use with vanilla, lemon, etc. Spread over cake with a palette knife.

Quantity guide for icing
When recipes specify an amount of icing such as '2 lb fondant, or royal, icing' this means the amount of sugar used in the icing. Where the basic recipe uses 1 lb icing sugar, you will need simply to double the quantities of all ingre-dients.

To calculate the weight of almond paste, add up the weight of the dry ingredients, ie. the ground almonds and sugar. The proportion of sugar to almonds can vary, but a general guide is to use equal amounts, the term 'sugar' usually

153

meaning half icing sugar and half caster sugar. If wished, however, you can increase the proportion of sugar, and for economy twice as much sugar as almonds can be used, although you will then need more egg to bind the mixture.

Nuts

To brown hazelnuts (already shelled) : do not blanch first but bake for 7-8 minutes in a moderate oven at 350°F or Mark 4, then rub briskly in a rough cloth to remove skin.

Almonds : buy them with their skins on. This way they retain their oil better. Blanching to remove the skins gives extra juiciness.

To blanch almonds : pour boiling water over the shelled nuts, cover the pan and leave until cool. Then the skins can be easily removed (test one with finger and thumb). Drain, rinse in cold water, and press skins off with fingers. Rinse nuts, dry thoroughly.

To brown blanched almonds : bake as for hazelnuts (above).

To chop almonds : first blanch, skin, chop and then brown them in the oven, if desired.

To shred almonds : first blanch, skin, split in two and cut each half lengthways in fine pieces. These can then be used as they are or browned quickly in the oven, with or without a sprinkling of caster sugar.

To flake almonds : first blanch, skin, and cut horizontally into flakes with a small sharp knife.

To grind almonds : first blanch, skin, chop and pound into a paste (use a pestle and mortar, or a grinder, or the butt end of a rolling pin). Home-prepared ground almonds taste much better than the ready-ground variety.

Pastry
French flan pastry (pâte sucrée)

4 oz plain flour
pinch of salt
2 oz butter
2 oz caster sugar
2-3 drops of vanilla essence
2 egg yolks

Note : 2 oz vanilla sugar may be used instead of caster sugar and vanilla essence.

Method
Sieve the flour with a pinch of salt on to a marble slab or pastry board, make a well in the centre and in it place the butter, sugar, vanilla essence and egg yolks. Using the fingertips of one hand only, pinch and work these last three ingredients together until well blended. Then draw in the flour, knead lightly until smooth.

Use as directed in the recipes.

Rich shortcrust pastry

8 oz plain flour
pinch of salt
6 oz butter
1 rounded dessertspoon caster sugar (for sweet pastry)
1 egg yolk
2-3 tablespoons cold water

Method
Sift the flour with a pinch of salt into a mixing bowl. Drop in the butter and cut it into the flour until the small pieces are well coated. Then rub them in with the fingertips until the mixture looks like fine breadcrumbs. Stir in the sugar, mix egg yolk with water, tip into the fat and flour and mix quickly with a palette knife to a firm dough.

Turn on to a floured board and

knead lightly until smooth. If possible, chill in refrigerator (wrapped in greaseproof paper, a polythene bag or foil) for 30 minutes before using.

Shortcrust pastry

8 oz plain flour
pinch of salt
4-6 oz butter, margarine, lard or shortening (one of the commercially-prepared fats), or a mixture of any two
3-4 tablespoons cold water

Method
Sift the flour with a pinch of salt into a mixing bowl. Cut the fat into the flour with a roundbladed knife and, as soon as the pieces are well coated with flour, rub in with the fingertips until the mixture looks like fine breadcrumbs.

Make a well in the centre, add the water (reserving about 1 tablespoon) and mix quickly with a knife. Press together with the fingers, adding the extra water, if necessary, to give a firm dough.

Turn on to a floured board, knead pastry lightly until smooth. Chill ·in refrigerator (wrapped in greaseproof paper, a polythene bag or foil) for 30 minutes before using.

Redcurrant jelly
It is not possible to give a specific quantity of redcurrants as the recipe is governed by the amount of juice made, which is variable.

Method
Wash the fruit and, without removing from the stems, put in a 7 lb jam jar or stone crock. Cover and stand in deep pan of hot water. Simmer on top of the stove or in the oven at 350°F or Mark 4, mashing the fruit a little from time to time, until all the juice is extracted (about 1 hour).

Then turn fruit into a jelly-bag, or double linen strainer, and allow to drain undisturbed overnight over a basin.

Watchpoint To keep the jelly clear and sparkling, do not try to speed up the draining process by forcing juice through ; this will only make the jelly cloudy.

Now measure juice. Allowing 1 lb lump or preserving sugar to each pint of juice, mix juice and sugar together, dissolving over slow heat. When dissolved, bring to the boil, boil hard for 3-5 minutes and skim with a wooden spoon. Test a little on a saucer : allow jelly to cool, tilt saucer and, if jelly is set, it will wrinkle. Put into jam jars, place small circles of greaseproof paper over jelly, label and cover with jam pot covers. Store in a dry larder until required.

Sugar syrup (for stock)
Dissolve 1 lb lump, or granulated, sugar in $\frac{1}{2}$ pint water and boil steadily, without stirring, until sugar thermometer reads 220°F. Allow syrup to cool, then store by pouring it into a large, clean and dry screwtop jar.

Vanilla sugar
Store a dry vanilla pod, or a few vanilla seeds, in a small jar of caster sugar. Keep well stoppered. This sugar may be used for flavouring cakes and custards.

Glossary

Dough Basic mixture of flour, liquid and fat for bread, scones, pastry.

Farl Traditional wedge shape of soda bread, scones etc. ; made by cutting circle of dough into four.

Glaze 1 To make shiny with egg, water and sugar, or milk. **2** Jam or fruit glaze for coating sweets and cakes.

Knead To work a dough with hands to required elasticity ; especially important in bread-making.

Prove To leave shaped dough for a short period of rising before baking. This is carried out in a slightly warmer place than for general rising ; for example over the stove or in a warming drawer, at about 80-85°F. Dough should be left for 10-15 minutes until it begins to swell.

Rise To leave kneaded dough to swell until double in bulk, when it is then ready for shaping. Dough should be left to rise in a greased bowl, covered with a damp cloth and set in a warm draught-free place. Temperature should be between 70-80°F.

Shortening Fat which when worked into flour gives a 'short', crisp quality to pastry / cakes. Fats with least liquid, e.g. lard, vegetable fat, contain most shortening power.

Index

157